# RICHARD III

RICARDVS · III · ANG · REX ·

Richard III by an unknown artist. By courtesy of
the *National Portrait Gallery, London.*

*William Shakespeare*

# RICHARD III

## Edward Burns

NORTHCOTE
BRITISH COUNCIL

In memory of Norman Rodway,
7th February 1922 – 13th March 2001

© Copyright 2006 by Edward Burns

First published in 2006 by Northcote House Publishers Ltd, Horndon House,
Horndon, Devon PL19 9NQ, United Kingdom.
Tel: +44 (01822) 810066 Fax: +44 (01822) 810034.

**British Library Cataloguing-in-Publication Data**
A catalogue record for this book is available from the British Library

ISBN 0-7463-0916-3

Typeset by PDQ Typesetting, Newcastle-under-Lyme
Printed and bound in the United Kingdom
by Athenaeum Press Ltd., Gateshead, Tyne & Wear

# Contents

# Illustrations

# Preface

Rather than presenting the text *Richard III* in this study in terms of a long past moment of authorial intent, I have tracked its mutations through its continuous and increasingly global stage history, and given the interpretations implied in its various cultural manifestations as much, if not more, emphasis than the commentaries of academic critics.

I make no apologies for this; it is, after all, in the nature of the beast. *Richard III* has, Frankenstein-like, (indeed, *Frankenstein*-like) escaped from its creator, into the wilderness of a disturbing psychological and historical terrain. And it is of the essence of the play that its performers have given it life in a way that commentators have more often than not been unable to. Consequently, references to productions (all the more recent ones seen by myself, live or on video) occur throughout the text, rather than being gathered together in a section on 'staging'. I have adopted the practice of labelling a production with its lead actor's and its director's name, the actor's coming first.

I have also, while indicating areas of academic debate, put references and citations in the endnotes to each section. This book aims to bridge the gap between the ordinary reader or play-goer and the student, and to offer something accessible and useful to both; summaries of critical controversy seem, in such a short book, best given concisely and apart. A full bibliography, with commentary, offers a route towards further reading.

# Acknowledgements

Thanks to Brian Hulme and Joanna Jellinek at Northcote House, for their work on a sadly delayed typescript. For that, my apologies. Thanks too, to Bernard Beatty, Cathy Rees, Barbara Smith, Karin Alcock and Janet Rothwell for saving the text and myself from an epic sequence of computer disasters. The staff of the Sydney Jones Library, Liverpool, and of the British Library, have been their usual helpful selves. Nick Davies, Alan Brookes and Lucy Kay read parts of an earlier version, and made the right kind of encouraging noises.

Special thanks are due to Suzie Quinsee, for combining a final rescue job on the disks with some sharp-eyed checking of quotes and format, and to Anne and John Barton, and Norman and Jane Rodway, for stimulating conversation and hospitality. Norman was the first Richard I saw, when at school, and to celebrate this and the set of personal connections that built up our friendship, I dedicate this book to his memory.

# Introduction

## MONSTERING RICHARD

There is a practice known to contemporary British journalists as 'monstering'. The editor of a 'tabloid' paper plans to focus on a notorious individual in order to increase their notoriety and so generate stories by portraying that individual as sensationally as possible. This involves provoking them and their associates into further statements and disclosures. Competing newspapers will join in and the more respectable 'broadsheets' will find a way of conveying all the stories generated in the guise of a critique of their colleagues' behaviour. In this process the line between legend, speculation and truth is blurred, becomes irrelevant; the effect is the creation of a kind of disposable folklore, at the expense of a living person.

The 'monstering' of the Duke of Gloucester (1452–85), crowned King Richard III in1483, has its origin in Shakespeare's sources, most notably in the life of Richard by Thomas More (probably written between 1510 and 1518), but the popularity of the play kept the legend alive. It has become the focus of a continuing, if perhaps academically marginalized controversy as to the extent of the historical Richard's 'guilt'.[1] There is a long-established Richard III society dedicated to clearing his name, several websites (I give addresses in my bibliography), and a number of speculative fictions like that of the detective story writer Josephine Tey, *The Daughter of Time* (1951), the daughter of time being, proverbially, truth.

The process of a revision of history whose aim is to declare Richard innocent began with Sir George Buck, in his *The History of the Life and Reigne of Richard III*, written in 1619 but not published until 1706.[2] Buck was a descendant of a Yorkist family;

1

his great-grandfather was executed after the battle of Bosworth, as a supporter of Richard. Perhaps it is a combination of support for the underdog and an unquenchable taste for conspiracy theory that has kept the pro-Richard camp going. Whenever I told a non-academic friend or acquaintance that I was working on this book, it was the forensic issue, the matter of evidence for Richard's guilt or innocence, that they wanted to talk about.

The crime of which Richard stands accused is of course the same crime which in the contemporary tabloid culture has lain behind the creation of the most obsessively represented 'monsters', the killing of children. I began work on this book in the furore surrounding the publication of an account of the crimes of Mary Bell, a woman, now a mother herself, who had, as a child, killed two small boys,[3] I continued working on it through a (false) rumour sweeping my neighbourhood that the two boys who killed the toddler Jamie Bulger were to be housed nearby, and as the tabloids compete in producing extreme and opposite images of Louise Woodward, the teenage nanny found guilty in the USA of the manslaughter of a baby, but freed after a review of conflicting evidence, and the serving of a minimal sentence. She denies the charge, but that didn't stop the banner headline 'First Class Baby Killer', her crime in this case being that she spent money on a first-class flight home to Britain. Richard is the original first-class baby killer. It is significant – and significant too for how we read Richard – that the contemporary figures I have named were children who killed children (it did Woodward no good that her supporters emphasized her immaturity). A child who kills another child is our culture's current icon of evil.

A vast number of illustrations, imaginative or based directly on stage productions, show that two visual images dominated the eighteenth- and nineteenth-century reception of the play: the active, solitary and deformed figure of Richard himself, often threatening the viewer of the picture, and so the audience, with a sword held aloft; and the paired princes, contrastingly still, in sleep or in death. The second of these images is created verbally in the play, but not presented on stage. As polarized images of evil and innocence, these have their resonances throughout English popular culture. Richard, as we shall see, pops up as Quilp in Charles Dickens's *The Old Curiosity Shop*, even as the puppet Mr Punch. The play belongs to that group of Shakespeare plays where culturally powerful images create a sense of familiarity which precedes our engagement with the text. This even carries over to specific performances – Sher's and Olivier's have created a kind of somatic memory that won't go away. Sher reports Kenneth Branagh telling him that he used to 'do' Olivier's Richard to amuse his school friends without either he or they knowing what it was.[4]

## TEXTS, EDITIONS, ADAPTATIONS

It's not only the historical Richard's reputation which has been subject to unending speculation and revision; what is labelled as the play *Richard III* in scholarly editions and in performance has always been a notably unstable object. Where it differs from others that enjoy the same degree of popular currency – *Romeo and Juliet* for example, or *Hamlet* – is that the original text presents problems in performance, which means that it is usually to some extent adapted and always heavily cut. All the major Shakespeare plays have a history of adaptation, but where the twentieth century saw all the others 'restored' to a more Shakespearean text, traditions of adapting *Richard III* have continued. It is as if the resonant situations and memorable scenes that have ensured its survival seem embedded in recalcitrant material, from which production must free them.

The problem is threefold. The play is very long – not only that, it feels long (in a way that *Hamlet*, with its forward moving 'thriller' structure, doesn't). It has, as Ernst Honigmann points out,[5] a structure based on repetition and doubling. It also has a very large cast, including five children, and not all of the characters – the queen's kindred, Richard's thugs, the weeping women – are easily distinguished one from the other by an audience. And the characters constantly refer back to complex actions that happened before the beginning of the play. It seems unlikely that the play has ever been performed complete. Some evidence that confusion, indecision and revision stem from its very earliest performances can be deduced from the relation of the single-volume texts of the play printed in Shakespeare's lifetime, the Quartos, to that printed in the Folio in 1623, some time after his death. This last text is fuller, not only in the length of speeches, but in the number of characters on stage at any one time, and is clearer in identifying who they are. But at the same time, if we see what is 'missing' from the Quartos as cuts, they are theatrically sensible ones. There are five Quartos, of which the first is most often used in modern editions; differences in the later ones are mostly local corrections. The Quartos include entertaining material – like Richard mocking Buckingham in the 'what's a clock' scene (IV.ii.8) – which are left out of the Folio; the Folio includes some powerful passages, like the Queen's address to the Tower, after she has been refused access to her imprisoned sons (IV.i.97–103), but also much exposition of events before the play starts, and much explanation, which is not always immediately dramatic. The Quartos' more economical deployment of Richard's henchmen and a certain openness as to how many duchesses and/or kindred of the queen are around at any point suggest a stage version of what is in the Folio a reading text. It makes for the presentation of a faster moving and clearer play; several commentators have argued for a theatrical provenance for the first Quarto, perhaps as a text devised for touring, perhaps pirated text, compiled from memory by actors for their own gain (given its accuracy and completeness, this would be a remarkable feat, even by Renaissance standards).[6]

Tastes in editing have changed somewhat in recent years. Where traditionally a situation like this would be solved by the creation of a composite text, in which the individual editor chooses, and argues for, what he or she thinks are the best, the most Shakespearean, choices, a respect for the differences between Quarto(s) and Folio, even a preference for the Quarto, seems to be emerging as a contemporary trend. So, while Antony Hammond's Arden (the text I use mainly here) and Ernst Honigmann's Penguin editions are composite texts, Peter Davison and Kristian Schmidt present the Quarto (the second, usefully, has the Folio on facing pages) and Gary Taylor's Oxford version is based on the Quarto, with the 'extra' Folio passages in an appendix. Later, I discuss one instance of where Quartos and Folio differ substantially in their presentation of a scene. At this point it is enough to observe that, even in a textually 'faithful' production, there is considerable instability in the object one is trying to be faithful to.

4

The adaptations of this material which all subsequent performances make to some degree or another tend to employ two apparently contradictory strategies, both traceable to the performing version prepared by Colley Cibber for his performances of the role in 1700. Though not uncontroversially successful in the role, he brought the play back to the stage in a highly influential form, and the attention he attracted prepared the way for David Garrick's spectacular success in 1741. One strategy is to bring in material from the earlier plays, particularly from the two soliloquies in *King Henry the Sixth, Part III* where Richard expounds his plan of action and establishes his character as the solitary assassin, the killer of Henry VI. Cibber makes Henry's death the centre of his first act, introducing Richard half-way through it with a truncated version of the opening soliloquy of *Richard III* and putting a cut-down version of the other great soliloquy from *King Henry the Sixth, Part III* near the beginning of his second act. Cibber's is an extremely free version, bringing in lines from other Shakespeare plays and new material. It is perhaps better judged as an independent piece than as a version of the Shakespeare. In these terms it is easy to see why it effectively replaced the unwieldy Shakespeare text on the stage. Cibber achieves not only greater clarity but also a kind of dry courtly wit that transposes the play effortlessly to the political intrigue of his own time. This is how he prefaces Elizabeth's reaction to Edward's death:

> SCENE *the Presence: Enter the Duke of* Buckingham *hastily, Lord Stanley meeting him.*
>
> *D. Buck.* Did you see the Duke?
> *L. Stan.* what D. [uke] my Lord?
> *D. Buck.* His Grace of *Gloucester,* did you see him?
> *L. Stan.* Not lately, my Lord – I hope no ill news.
> *D. Buck.* The worst that heart e're bore, or tongue can utter.
> *Edward the* King! his Royal Brother's Dead.
> *L. Stan.* 'Tis sad indeed...
>
> . . . . . . . . . .
>
> Did the King, my Lord, make any mention
> Of a Protector for his Crown and Children?
> *D. Buck.* He did, Duke *Richard* has the care of both.
> *L. Stan.* That sad news you are afraid to tell him too *[aside]*

5

*D. Buck* He'll spare no toile, I'm sure to fill his Place!
*L. Stan.* Pray Heav'n he's not too diligent! *[aside]*[7]

This kind of writing acts well; Cibber manages the dry ruthless tone of aristocratic power-broking with a certain finesse. The same effect is aimed for but less securely achieved in Ian McKellen's rewrite of the play for the film, directed by Richard Loncraine, in which he starred. Other equally bold attempts have been made to clarify the play. Al Pacino's film *Looking for Richard* intercuts, in about equal proportions, performances of key scenes from the play, shot on approximately apt locations and lit in a moody (and budget-flattering) Caravaggiesque style, with discussions between the actors and interviews with academic and theatrical authorities; Pacino's starting point is the text's frustrating mix of theatrical power and narrative incomprehensibility. A production at the Liverpool Everyman in the 1980s by Tim Albery with Paul Jesson as Richard presented a heavily cut version of *King Henry the Sixth, Part III* as the first half of the evening. *Richard III* followed in an equally heavily cut text, both pieces presented austerely, in battle dress, with Brechtian captions labelling the action as a sequence of betrayals.

The more usual twentieth-century equivalent to embedding the soliloquies and Henry's murder in the play, as Cibber did, is to perform it as part of a cycle incorporating cut or, as in the case of the BBC Shakespeare production (Cook/Howell), complete versions of the *Henry VII* plays, or perhaps even, as in the case of the Royal Shakespeare Company's *The Wars of the Roses* (1964), the BBC's, *The Age of Kings* (1960) and the English Shakespeare Company's history sequence (1988), the whole historical narrative from the second Richard through to the third. The ESC performances shape the material into an 'epic' theatrical event, where the two-part adaptation of the *Henry VI* plays was performed in the morning and afternoon, with *Richard III* in the evening. In the interest of the narrative clarity of a 'cycle' presentation, the beginning of Michael Bogdanov's ESC production sacrificed this most famous of openings in English drama for a wittily conceived cocktail party, at which Hastings chattily introduced the audience to the individual members of a now hypocritically celebratory group, in a buttonholing narration of their past crimes. The RSC in 1988 compressed the *Henry VI* material into another two-parter, *The Plantagenets*, and after performing them apart from *Richard III* at the Swan in Stratford-upon-Avon, added *Richard,* with many of the same actors continuing their roles, to a main-house revival of the originally smaller-scale diptych.

*The Wars of the Roses,* the adaptation of *Henry VI* and *Richard III* made for the RSC by Peter Hall and John Barton in 1964 and later televised, was highly influential in its instatement of *Richard III* as the climax of a longer sequence. This form of presentation has been hailed as a rediscovery of the play, to rank with Irving's final, late nineteenth-century abandonment of the Cibber text. It certainly becomes something different when put in this context.[8] Even actors, Antony Sher for example, who perform in a single-play presentation, and who initially resist the idea of 'homework', have worked aspects of their performances out from an awareness of the story as the earlier plays tell it. In this study, I will discuss the play both as a free-standing piece and as the culmination of a dramatized historical, even psychological, process. To do so, as we shall see, is to acknowledge what the play has become, rather than to reconstruct what it was for an 'original' audience.

Twentieth-century critical writing on the play has been dominated, at least in the years after the second world war, by the controversy as to whether Shakespeare's sequence of history plays amount to a 'Tudor epic' which culminates in the God-ordained instatement of Richard's adversary, Richmond, as King Henry VII, and so in the validation of the Tudor dynasty of which Elizabeth, elderly and childless at the time of the writing of the play, was obviously the last. I will deal with this as a scholarly debate later in the book. The alternatives to this view, which largely stems from the work of E. M. Tillyard and Lily B. Campbell[9] are that the plays are either self-contained, or subversive of an idea of historical progress, or both.[10] Barton and Hall, in forming the RSC, aimed to make Shakespearean production in Britain more attuned both to scholarly trends and to the political life of the contemporary world. Their reinstatement of the less well-known history plays into the Shakespearean repertoire may have stemmed from Tillyard's work, but operated in reaction to it. Jan Kott's *Shakespeare Our Contemporary,* cited by Hall at the beginning of rehearsals,[11] presents history as a process, but an essentially meaningless one, a 'grand mechanism'. This view has more theatrical potential than the sense of the plays as a providential 'Tudor epic'; to try to instate that would be to risk turning the plays into a museum piece, not simply in alienating them from the 'contemporary' in the name of 'authenticity', but in denying much of their basic energy by emphasizing pattern and unambiguous moralization at the expense of violence and irony. When *Richard* is performed alone, the issue, till then a rather confusing 'background' to the play, becomes visible with the arrival of Richmond. I will return to this in my last chapter, in exploring the significance of this play's final moments.

In terms of strict authenticity, the arrangement of the plays as a political 'cycle', whatever the politics of the arrangers, is as much a form of adaptation as the rewritings that bring in material from *Henry the Sixth, Part III* to flesh out an individual portrait. Shakespeare cannot have envisaged, let alone seen, the plays performed in this way in his own lifetime. Though the Folio presents them in this way, it could only have been Shakespeare's conception if he were engaged in a somewhat quixotic private aesthetic project, of which original audiences and readers could not have been aware, given the relative anonymity of Elizabethan playwrights, the casualness of play-going as a habit and the lack of a tradition of 'serial' presentation. Commentators have often – indeed, more often than not – assumed that the history plays were presented as a cycle, on the analogy of the Corpus Christi cycles,[12] but there is no evidence that this ever happened – and one would assume there would be evidence for a theatrical event on this scale. Elizabethan audiences knew their history from a wide range of sources; memories or half memories of plays some years old would be related to chronicles, to popular memory, to oral history and to the evidence of the history of London in its monuments, buildings and traditions. *Richard III* draws on all these. A combination of lack of such historical knowledge, and a linear cause-and-effect notion of history make the 'cycle' presentation attractive to us; to the Elizabethans it would have been unnecessary, as well as economically inconceivable.

The alternative to adaptation by addition is clarification by cutting, often drastically, to the extent of excising complete characters. The early eighteenth century establishes the principle of a remaking of the play as a portrait of Richard, in which all else takes a second place. A mid-twentieth-century tendency to present the play as a broad political canvas has been superseded, in Britain at least, by a return to this earlier idea of the play as star vehicle, as the psychological study of a charismatic psychopath. Antony Sher's performance in Bill Alexander's RSC production is at the root of this as a theatrical trend. The critical tradition which this echoes has been less academically respectable, despite Freud's exploration of the play, largely because it has been seen as limited to character study. Freud himself was more interested in the audience's response.[13] A developing vein of feminist writing on the play reinstates the psychological reading in exposing, often excitingly, psychological and sexual issues as more than simply a matter of individual psychopathology.

Queen Margaret, the chief memorialist of the earlier events, and the choric, perhaps prophetic observer of Richard's career has been the most spectacular casualty of cuts inflicted on the play in a 'psychological', as opposed to a 'historical', reading. She was left out of Cibber's adaptation, to be reinstated in the nineteenth century, only to disappear in the Olivier film. The Sher/Alexander version eventually cut Margaret, on its Australian tour. In an early performance seen by the current writer, the distinguished actress playing the role had seemed out of place and ill at ease, as the logic of the production allowed her no very clear relation to action or audience. Her first scene, according to Sher's account of the rehearsals, was one to which the performers never felt that they had found a solution.[14] The McKellen/Loncraine film cuts her, but combines lines and aspects of the character with those of the Duchess of York (Maggie Smith).

In all these versions, the play was reshaped to focus more clearly on, and to make more sense of, Richard as an individual. The balance of emphasis of the post-Cibber adaptations – which can be broadly classified as psychological *or* political – can be seen in the relative weight accorded to the Duchess of York and to Margaret. Margaret is important in a production which stresses a historical or religious perspective. The Chkivadze/Sturua production, from Rustavelli in then Soviet Georgia (an enormous success in Edinburgh and London in 1979, and as much a benchmark for future directors and actors as Olivier's) had Margaret on stage throughout, often reading out stage directions, acting as a kind of stage-manager and prompt.[15] The Lindsay/Moshinsky production had her re-emerge at the very end of the play to face Richmond, a somewhat puzzling effect, but one that emphasized her perverse permanence in the world of the play. But the reshaping of the Sher/Alexander and McKellen/Loncraine versions layers a popularized twentieth-century psychology on to the star-centred adaptations of Cibber, Garrick and Olivier. The Duchess of York edges Margaret out; we are less interested in history than in meeting the psycho's mum.

The psychological version, from Cibber on, adapts more freely, is less concerned with locating the action in a believable political or historical context and will tend to drastically prune back the cast. The 'political' will draw on the preceding plays, and reinstate 'minor' figures like the Scrivener or the Citizens, an important part of the play's argument about history, and resist cutting down the early court scenes, Hastings's journey towards his last council meeting, Richard's 'courtship' of Elizabeth, and other scenes which present the protagonist as part of a larger process. If we were trying to reconstitute the play to its Elizabethan form, it would be unhelpful to make this distinction. Neither the discipline of psychology nor the idea of an objective, materialist analysis of history would have been available to an early audience. But they form the cultural context of later reception of the play, and so are the condition of its adaptation and performance, the creative distortions which mark its theatrical life.

The play has fed into the British historical imagination, images and ideas which seem to detach themselves from an unwieldy text. This, and the fact that its survival on stage has depended on adaptation and mutation, gives us a much more unstable object of attention than we would have in dealing with any other major Shakespeare play. But this is a token of theatrical vitality, and of an imaginative conception that breaks loose, Frankenstein-like, from the confines of critical practice and piety towards an integral text. In this study I want to pay attention to both this imaginative after-life and what it tells us about the play's concerns, and the detail of the surviving texts themselves. A visual convention of the Renaissance, that of the anamorphic image, offers its own way into the idea of distortion and deformity, an idea I shall use to structure my investigation of the play. Where contemporary 'monstering' loses truth, the anamorphic image depends on a notion of 'true' perspective, which it instates for us by drawing us into its opposite.

## THE ANAMORPHIC IMAGE

Holbein's painting *The Ambassadors,* in the National Gallery in London, is a portrait of two figures, one of whom commissioned it and took it back with him to his home, the (with an accidental pun) 'Chateau de Polissy'. The policy of the 'ambassadors' was aimed at a resolution of the Reformation, of the Lutheran secession from the Catholic church, and, as the excellent book which accompanied the exhibition of the newly restored picture at the National Gallery explains, many of the emblems in the picture figure the division the 'ambassadors' were attempting to close.[16] At the front, famously, is a distorted skull, visible only as a skull if one stands to the side of the picture and looks at it aslant. The restoration has reconstructed the nose bone, so the illusion is more convincing than in the version of the painting we used to know. Less famously, there is a crucifix in the far right-hand corner. We can only see half of it, and then only because the green curtain behind the two deliberately posed figures has (presumably accidentally) started to fall away. It is described as silver in the catalogue, but it looks to me more like pewter, or some other base metal. The crucifix is, as the book puts it 'the last thing in the picture the viewer will find'. If one is in the position, in front of the actual painting, to see the skull as a skull one cannot see the crucifix at all. When one looks at the crucifix, which, as Stephen Greenblatt puts it in a celebrated reading of the painting, possesses 'a certain cultic imperviousness to the corrosive effects of anamorphosis'[17] the skull becomes a vaguely luminous blur.

So, in its presence, the picture dramatizes us as spectators – we are conscious of moving around, taking position, seeing partially, worrying that we are missing something. Importantly, the picture is constructed to offer us a choice – skull or crucifix?

11

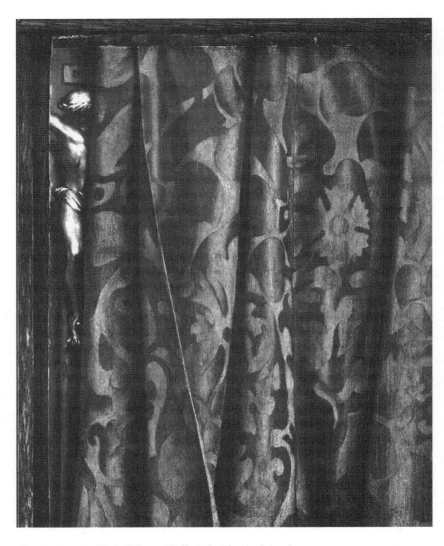

Illustration 1    Detail from Holbein's *The Ambassadors*

– the mortality that defines us as human, and which we focus on by standing where we have only an oblique view of the mundanely, outwardly confident, but oh-so-tense 'ambassadors' and lose the crucifix, or the redemption in Christ, which, in a focus on the crucifix takes us to the right-hand corner of the picture, above the earthly protagonists of a risky politics, and away from being able to 'read' the skull altogether.

*Richard III* may well, if we accept Ernst Honigmann's argument of its – and the developing Shakespeare's – indebtedness to the work of another of Holbein's sitters, Thomas More, have a conceptual and historical link to the representational strategies of the humanist culture of some decades earlier.[18] We can see Shakespeare's reflection on this kind of humanism, and on the contradictions within it, as the source of his most powerful theatrical effects. More, in his unfinished *Life* of Richard made him almost non-human, a monster. A monster is a thing to be looked at, on the understanding that its looks bewray its nature. But we are embarrassed when we look at monsters, in the sense that we are aware of ourselves looking (so embarrassed, burdened down, with a sense of ourselves). We don't know where we stand, where we should stand, how or whether we should let the monster look back at us when we are looking at – it? More also employs a range of rhetorical strategies to make the reader aware of the complexities and dangers of response to this kind of material. Shakespeare, like Holbein, seems to me to put within the image we confront markers of different kinds of looking, different foci of attention.

The visual tradition which Holbein is working out of was relatively recent. The fashion for the anamorphic image, the image that changes shape according to the angle from which it is viewed, was developed by Leonardo da Vinci during his stay in France, and this is where Jean de Dinteville, one of the two 'ambassadors' may have encountered it, and so commissioned Holbein to include such a thing in his portrait.[19] There is a portrait of the adolescent Edward IV, at Windsor Castle, which to see as a face more or less in proportion (I can't do it without his retaining a Pinocchio nose – is this the point?) you have to look through a hole in the side of the frame. An engraving of the Emperor Ferdinand, illustrated in the National Gallery catalogue, observes a similar convention; around the distorted face of the

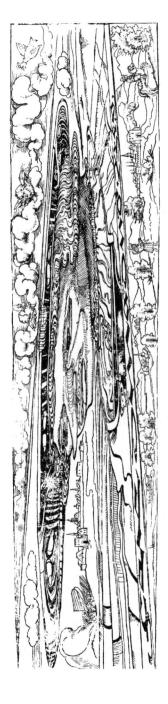

Illustration 2  E. Schön, anamorphic image of the Emperor Ferdinand

14

ruler is an oval frame which, if we adopt the right perspective, should become circular, and around the frame is a cosy northern European landscape with, in both cases, an unthreateningly small town, a couple of cheerful peasants and a church. But of course, if we are to see the ruler as himself, we lose (as in the Holbein we lose either crucifix or skull) the country he rules. It disappears. So what is the ruler 'himself'? It is his head, presented in a medallion, a convention to celebrate 'honour' by detaching not only ruler from ruled, but head from body, a convention that migrates from Roman to Renaissance Italian art, and then, somewhat uneasily, to the north.

*Richard III* seems to me to have a similar effect. We are aware of the difficulties of perspective (we are also aware of more than one detached head), and the uneasiness of spectatorship (especially as we seem to be, potentially at least, spectators to a sequence of executions). In this sense the focus on the central figure is not so much an invitation to a psychological case study, a forensic attempt to understand a monstrous psychology, as a test in the alignment of our gaze and our judgement, a psychological investigation, if of anything, of us. Richard is an engrossing puzzle, a haunting anamorph. And the play around him, like the details in the Holbein picture, or the landscapes in the royal portraits, changes in focus as we struggle to find a standpoint from which to see him whole. Larger structures, political or religious, disappear, like the crucifix in Holbein's picture, or Margaret in the adaptations, when we allow Richard to dictate our position to us.

*Richard III* can be described as a text made up of, and conveying, distortions. Of course, to say that something is distorted is to imply that there is a 'proper' shape that it *ought* to have; from that point of view, the play can be read conservatively, as showing the reality of order and harmony, and an accessible idea of historical truth, by presenting its opposite. One of the things, as we have seen and shall see again, that scholars have argued has been lost in the cultural reception, the 'distortion' of the play, is the sense of a seriously imagined framework of Christian providentialism, by virtue of which Richmond's taking of the throne is unironically celebrated and the play is an illumination and resolution of the preceding chaos, a revelation that all was not necessarily lost and that divine order had prevailed. On the other hand, the play can be taken to question the existence of that order, to undermine our certainty that there is such a thing as historical truth. By pulling us into its sequence of distortions, by confusing us to the extent that we lose our bearings, our sense of proportion, it makes imaginatively close to us, with both enjoyable and discomfiting results, the emotional space of destructive libidinous energy which Richard inhabits. Or perhaps, most involvingly, it places us in a hall of mirrors where we just give up on tracing what is a distortion and what not. The play is uniquely entertaining, and the energy it liberates is more to do with these last kinds of response than with the 'proper' or 'correct' readings of events it may only really tease us with. For us now the play is inevitably both a highly structured historically investigable Elizabethan text, and the unleashing, via the theatre, of an energetic individual myth.

I have used the idea of distortion as the starting point for a sequence of five sections, within which I will consider the text of the play and its realization on the stage and in other media, so that the one may illuminate the other. I have put the topics in an order which allows me to keep broadly to the narrative of the play, in order to provide a readable introduction to its action and concerns. I will concentrate discussion of individual characters other than Richard within discussion of the act where they seem most important.

Firstly, distortion of *the body* as announced by Richard's entrance at the very start of the play, and his reflection on this. His wooing of Lady Anne puts an erotic context around what he has presented initially in terms of an exclusion from the libidinous atmosphere surrounding his brother Edward. The meanings that culturally accrue to deformation and disability are made play of in the drama, but the very idea that Richard was 'deformed' is itself a distortion of *history*. Events and responsibility for them are endlessly recounted by characters in the play, which also, expanding on its sources, meditates on the processes of historical memory and of the recording of history. Margaret seems to instate in the play the sense that history has a pattern, across which we can look both backward and forward, but we may question her power and be sceptical as to whether history is divinely ordained and controlled. Richard forces events into the pattern he wishes through an exploitation of the power of *plays and players,* and the play has been a powerful text, particularly in the twentieth century, for considering the part propaganda and the staging of events have in political change. His ally here is Buckingham, who is both stage-manager and audience, and on whom Richard seems to rely for the approval he has been denied elsewhere. The fourth act, and my fourth section, is concerned with *marriage and the family,* in a context where politics drives but is also driven by patterns of family relationship, and where, in the murder of the princes, the focus is on the idea of childhood innocence, but, contradictorily, also on Richard's own childlikeness. Finally, the appearance of the ghosts allows a retrospective consideration of the play; *mirrors and shadows* provide ways of knowing the self, but at a cost which their iconographic associations, and their history as psychological metaphors, encode.

# 1

## The Body

The play opens with startling immediacy. In a shared present tense, established with the opening syllable – 'now' – we are confronted by a figure whose body speaks to us before he opens his mouth. No other Shakespeare character – except perhaps Falstaff, or the 'translated' Bottom – has such an instantly recognizable physical appearance. As the play goes on, we are invited to read, to puzzle at, this anomalous body. Richard's first speech presents his physical shape in terms of the exclusion it forces on him, and he presents as exclusion from relationships with women.

> But I, that am not shap'd for sportive tricks,
> Nor made to court an amorous looking-glass;
> I, that am rudely stamp'd, and want love's majesty
> To strut before a wanton ambling nymph:
> I, that am curtail'd of this fair proportion,
> Cheated of feature by dissembling Nature,
> Deform'd, unfinish'd, sent before my time
> Into this breathing world scarce half made up –
> And that so lamely and unfashionable
> That dogs bark at me, as I halt by them –
> Why, I, in this weak piping time of peace,
> Have no delight to pass away the time,
> Unless to spy my shadow in the sun,
> And descant on mine own deformity.
> And therefore, since I cannot prove a lover
> To entertain these fair well-spoken days,
> I am determined to prove a villain,
> And hate the idle pleasures of these days.

(I.i.14–31)

In this he contrasts himself to his brother King Edward IV, 'this son of York' of the second line of the play, as 'love's majesty'

18

points up in its reference to kingship. Edward was a notorious womanizer, whose most famous mistress was the city woman Jane Shore. She is alluded to in the play text, and was very much part of the story as the audience would already know it, but she has no lines in the play, and is only present on stage if a director chooses to make her so.

In a psychological reading of the play, Richard's 'deformity' – to use a term which a modern reader may prefer to replace with 'disability', but which the play, at this early stage, has Richard use of himself – can be invoked as the motivation of his actions. In the reading of the plays as a historical cycle, Richard's deformity can be read as a metaphor not simply for individual depravity, but for a deformation of the body politic; according to a standard Renaissance analogy, the working state can be imaged as a healthy well-proportioned body, but this has been lost in the 'deformity' and 'unnaturalness' of civil conflict. The deformed Richard is an affront to the Renaissance mapping of the cosmos on a perfect young male body, its model of proportion and order;[1] he is a visible emblem of the chaos of late medieval history.

The Russian theorist Bakhtin develops a contrast between the medieval and the Renaissance in terms of this image of the body. In the earlier period the grotesque is celebrated, unfettered; gargoyle-like figures are part of our image of the medieval, largely because the visual arts of that period persistently present such figures as marginal (often in the literal sense of decoration on the margins of texts) but in other ways central, as pointing to the chaotic physicality of human life. In Bakhtin's equation at least, the medieval, the disorderly, is also linked to the female.[2] In this reading, Richard produces, in his relation to women, the sense of a dangerous sexual carnival. Perhaps the deformed and the female are equated from the point of view of the humanist, male-centred cosmos. The programme of the Rodway/Hands production had as its cover image a distortion of the Leonardo da Vinci 'Renaissance Man' – a recurrent image in RSC productions and a visual leitmotif of the season (1970) in which Richard was performed.[3]

The link between physical deformity, moral 'monstering' and political propaganda is best demonstrated by a presentation of Thomas More's influential but historically unverifiable description of Richard. More's history is based on Latin models,

19

particularly Tacitus and Suetonius, and takes over from them the convention of the 'vignette', a character sketch of the historical figure in which physical characteristics, moral judgements and hints of action are presented together, and are by implication continuous with one another.[4] This is his description of Richard. Its starting point is a comparison with his brothers Edward and George Duke of Clarence:

> Richard ... was in wit and courage equal with either of them, in body and prowess far under them both, little of stature, ill-featured of limbs, crook-backed, his left shoulder much higher than his right, hard favoured of visage, and such as in states called warlike, in other men otherwise. He was malicious, wrathful, envious, and from afore his birth, ever froward. It is for truth reported, that the Duchess his mother had so much ado in her travail, that she could not be delivered of him uncut: and that he came into the world with the feet forward, as men be born outward, and (as the fame runneth) also not untoothed, whether men of hatred report above the truth, or else that nature changed her course in his beginning, which in the course of his life many things unnaturally committed. None evil captain was he in the war, as to which his disposition was more meetly than for peace. Sundry victories had he, and sometime overthrows, but never in default as for his own person, either of hardiness or politic order. Free was he called of dispense, and somewhat above his power liberal, with large gifts he got him unsteadfast friendship, for which he was fain to pill and spoil in other places, and get him steadfast hatred. He was close and secret, a deep dissimuler, lowly of countenance, arrogant of heart, outwardly companiable where he inwardly hated, not letting to kiss whom he thought to kill: dispitious and cruel, not for evil will always, but ofter for ambition, and either for the surety or increase of his estate. Friend and foe was much what indifferent, where his advantage grew, he spared no man's death, whose life withstood his purpose. He slew with his own hands King Henry the Sixth, being prisoner in the Tower, as men constantly say ...[5]

This is worth looking at closely, as most aspects of this description are invoked in the play. The moral and the physical are subtly linked in More's language; 'little' and 'ill' in ordinary English usage have currency both as physical and as moral descriptions. Later, 'lowly of countenance, arrogant of heart' has the same effect; metaphor makes the physical and the moral continuous with each other. That is the point of the kind of writing in which More is engaged, and which Shakespeare echoes; it presents the source and meaning of events as a matter of individual character and presents that 'character' as substantial and coherent as if it were physical fact.

The theatrical panache of the play's opening instates an invitation to read Richard's visual appearance as its opening gambit, its challenge to the audience. In beginning, not with the crowded court or a ceremonial scene, but with the entrance of an individual, identified in some way as an outsider, *Richard III* is more typical of the plays of Christopher Marlowe than of Shakespeare's Elizabethan plays.[6] The solitary individual in Marlowe – Barabbas (a Jew), Gaveston (an extravagant homosexual), Faustus (a scholar) – is realized visually as an outsider – in costume, make-up, solitary situation. In *Dr Faustus* and *The Jew of Malta* Marlowe uses a chorus figure to introduce the protagonist, to underline and to account for his difference. This is not the case with Richard. He enters as chorus to himself. We have a visual image, an icon, before we hear a voice, and not only does he establish himself before we see the character of highest social status, his brother the king (which is in itself unconventional for a play of this period), but he speaks of himself first, to pre-empt anyone's speaking of him, their putting a frame around him.

Productions have differed as to the extent of physical distortion. The Sher/Alexander was probably the most spectacular in a realization of the deformity/disability that made expensive use of prosthetics developed for modern horror films to create a kind of new creature – though this aspect, a major drain on the production budget was disappointing to Sher in being realized on a filmic, 'close-up' scale.[7] It was shown off in a historically derived addition to the text, where, at the end of the first half of the show, Richard and Anne were, with their backs to the audience, stripped to the waist in order to be anointed as part of the ritual of their coronation. But it was the intense exploration by Sher of animal movement and his study of real disability which created Richard's body.[8] Sher has been widely credited with finding a new somatic image to effectively replace that of the highly successful and much parodied Laurence Olivier film. Sher's Richard was crippled to the extent of reliance on crutches which created the visual image of a spider in

Illustration 3   Norman Rodway as Richard III and Ian Richardson as Buckingham in the 1970 RSC production

shockingly rapid and disturbingly unpredictable motion. At one point he was to be found crouched arachnoid-like on one of the tombs, breathing rhythmically, an effect made the more inhuman in the continuation of the breathing rhythm down the crutches and flowing sleeves that stood in for the spider's non-human plenitude of limbs. The extent of Richard's disability was such that – while it made the cry for 'a horse' the more compelling, as there seemed no other way Richard could survive the battle – it made nonsense of Richard's role in the earlier plays as the fiercest and most competent fighter. Knocking his crutches from under him seemed all too obvious and easy an option. Sher's account of his preparation for the role records this as the first objection of almost anyone to whom he reveals his concept.[9] It could not possibly have worked had one been invited to cross-reference this figure with the character in the earlier plays. In the McKellen/Loncraine the deformity is discreet, the character's body, and by implication his mind, just slightly, if significantly, twisted off-beam. McKellen's hooded, sour face creates most of the effect. Ian Holm and Anton Lesser, in 'cycle' presentations, were in this tradition, if more plausibly attractive; Holm in particular was almost pretty, a wide-eyed sharper who could have come out of a play by Joe Orton.

The entrance has become so renowned – Sher comments that it is now almost impossible for an actor and jokingly suggested to his director that they should cut it[10] – that directors and actors feel they have to run some variant on it. Many productions have the court on stage, to define Richard's isolation against them. In the Loncraine film McKellen, perhaps rather unfortunately, given his role as gay rights campaigner, beckons us to follow him into a gents' toilet. In Adrian Noble's production Anton Lesser dashed out (on 'But I') from a group of gold-clad court revellers into a white spotlight that cast a double shadow. In the Troughton/Pimlott version too, 'But I' is the point at which the break is made between ironic public speechifying and embittered soliloquy. Troughton entered through a hesitantly opened door at the back of the set, a more timid Quasimodo-ish figure than most Richards. He is interrupted by the giggling, gaudily dressed court figures, who run across a gantry at the back of the set, and, apparently scared, dives back through his door, only to emerge with jester's hat and rattle to act up the first part of his

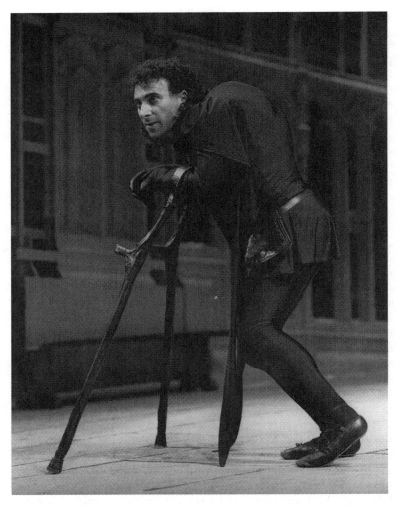

Illustration 4    Anthony Sher as Richard III in the 1984 RSC production

speech to the jeering courtiers in the tradition of Mr Punch. Until 'But I...', where the courtiers leave and he begins to share his personal bitterness with the audience; a retreat into a dangerous singularity.

*Henry the Sixth, Part III* gives us the clearest description we get in the plays of the extent and nature of Richard's physical deformity. This figure, Shakespeare's earlier Richard, takes one step further the revenge motivation of Marlowe's outsider protagonists. He has a grudge against nature itself. His earlier soliloquy in *Henry the Sixth, Part III* comes after he has witnessed his brother Edward's wooing of Lady Grey, the Queen Elizabeth of the later play. It expresses a complex hostility which seems to go beyond either the misogyny or the sibling rivalry that both inform it.

> Ay, Edward will use women honorably.
> Would he were wasted, marrow, bones and all,
> That from his loins no hopeful branch may spring
> To cross me from the golden time I look for!
> .    .    .    .    .    .    .    .    .    .
> My eye's too quick, my heart o'erweens too much,
> Unless my hand and strength could equal them.
> Well say there is no other kingdom then for Richard;
> What other pleasure can the world afford?
> I'll make my heaven in a lady's lap,
> And deck my body in gay ornaments
> And witch sweet ladies with my words and looks.
> O miserable thought! And more unlikely
> Than to accomplish twenty golden crowns!
> Why, Love forswore me in my mother's womb
> And for I should not deal in her soft laws,
> She did corrupt frail Nature with some bribe,
> To shrink mine arm up like a wither'd shrub;
> To make an envious mountain on my back,
> Where sits deformity to mock my body;
> To shape my legs of an unequal size,
> To disproportion me in every part,
> Like to a chaos or an unlick'd bear-whelp
> That carries no impression like the dam.
>
> (III.ii. 124–62)

The soliloquy from *Henry the Sixth, Part III* registers deformity clearly but as a problem in the eroticized atmosphere that

Edward's victory creates; it has to be compensated for by the attainment of power:

> And am I then a man to be belov'd?
> O monstrous fault to harbor such a thought!
> Then, since this earth affords no joy to me
> But to command, to check, to o'erbear such
> As are of better person than myself,
> I'll make my heaven to dream upon the crown
> And whiles I live, t'account this world but hell,
> Until this head my misshap'd trunk that bears this head
> Be round impaled with a glorious crown.
>
> (III.ii.163–71)

Richard's physical oddity is linked to unpredictable speed, not impediment, of motion and decision – 'My eye's too quick, my heart o'erweens too much...' (III.ii.144). Richard's very disability is the token of physicality, of an amoral energy that is frustrated in ordinary social and sexual contexts, and which needs to be used up.

Richard's next soliloquy in this earlier play, after his killing of Henry VI, is another, slightly different, attempt to account for his physical form. The new Richard, the one that we see as if fully formed at the start of *Richard III* when we see the play performed alone, is conceived at the climax of *Henry the Sixth, Part III* by his own deed, his killing of King Henry, and by Henry's narrative of his assassin's monstrous birth; the two coincide at the very moment of stabbing. Henry is by now established in the play as a prophet, perhaps also a kind of magician.

> The owl shriek'd at thy birth, an evil sign;
> The night-crow cried, aboding luckless time;
> Dogs howl'd and hideous tempests shook down trees;
> The raven rook'd her on the chimney's top
> And chatt'ring pies in dismal discords sung;
> Thy mother felt more than a mother's pain
> And yet brought forth less than a mother's hope,
> To wit, an indigested and deformed lump,
> Not like the fruit of such a goodly tree.
> Teeth hadst thou in thy head when thou wast born
> To signify thou cam'st to bite the world;
> And if the rest be true, which I have heard,
> Thou cam'st –

GLOUCESTER    I'll hear no more: die, prophet, in thy speech:
                                                                  [*Stabs him*]
For this among the rest, was I ordained.
    KING HENRY    Ay, and for much more slaughter after this
    GLOUCESTER    Down, down to hell, and say I sent thee thither –
                                                            [*Stabs him again*]

.    .    .    .    .    .    .    .    .

I that have neither pity, love, nor fear,
Indeed 'tis true that Henry told me of,
For I have often heard my mother say
I came into the world with my legs forward.
Had I not reason, think ye, to make haste
And seek their ruin that usurp'd our right?
The midwife wonder'd and the women cried,
'O Jesus bless us, he is born with teeth!'
And so I was, which plainly signified
That I should snarl, and bite, and play the dog.
Then, since the heavens have shaped my body so,
Let hell make crook'd my mind to answer it.
[I had no father, I am like no father;][11]
I have no brother, I am like no brother;
And this word 'love', which greybeards call divine,
Be resident in men like one another,
And not in me: I am myself alone.

                                                        (V.vi.44–83)

This scene is a transaction. Henry gives Richard an identity
and he accepts it. The moment of killing Henry seals the
transaction; it interrupts the narrative at the very moment of the
telling of the murderer's birth. Actors can of course play this as a
provocation to Richard to lose his temper, a masochistic taunting
by a rather less than saintly Henry, in which he brings on his
own martyrdom and the damnation of his opponent. This
makes sense, but Richard's calm recapitulation of the narrative
marks the scene as a kind of ritual. In *Richard III* the wounds on
Henry's corpse reopen, when Richard confronts Anne in the
funeral procession, as 'mouths' that speak of their knowledge of
Richard's guilt. In joining in with Henry's narrative, Richard is
assenting in a fiction, and making it true. He is also giving it
meaning. The 'indigested and deformed lump' is without
meaning, even the meanings we ordinarily read onto the
human form, but when Richard, in the act of stabbing, says 'For

this among the rest, was I ordained', he invests the visual icon of the persona he has accepted with a dynamic significance, an 'ordained' validity with a supernatural, perhaps even a divine, source. He is a visual chaos whose inner logic is its termination of the dynastic squabbles from which it stems.

Colley Cibber introduced a version of this scene into his *The Tragical History of Richard III*, where it stayed in performing versions well into the nineteenth century. Some of the lines are incorporated into the first soliloquy in Olivier's film.[12] This is all understandable, if audience and actor want to know where Richard is 'coming from'. The soliloquies provide a coherent (if twisted) spine to a play whose action otherwise proceeds through a bewildering sequence of reversals. It is possible to read the working out of the character across the *Henry VI* plays as a psychological development. This earlier Richard certainly changes, grows; the later play takes the end point of that development, the solitary self-defining killer of King Henry, and develops it in the sense of opening it out, of unfolding its implications. But there is no sense in the play that we are to see Richard as psychologically 'deformed' by his physical disability in itself, or as stigmatized in any way as monstrous by his family, who are consistently affectionate. York is among Shakespeare's better parents, and Richard's friendship with his brothers carries over, in their minds at least, to our play; the effect of Clarence's disbelief at his murderers' insistence at Richard's responsibility for his imminent death conveys a particular pathos.

It is Richard's enemies who give him his identity, or rather, read his physical appearance back to him as his identity in every other sense. This singles him out from the group of brothers, with whom in the earlier plays he always enters. Within that group, among York's supporters, his physical appearance is unmentioned. In the *Henry VI* plays, Richard emerges almost casually as part of an increasingly confused and crowded canvas. His behaviour is not that much different to anyone else's. Indeed, until the end of *Henry the Sixth, Part III* he seems in many ways more likeable than most; more honest at least, and loyal to his uncomplicatedly clannish family. Margaret and Clifford behave more violently and cruelly than has Richard at this stage in his career, but in their case the play stresses a contradiction between look and nature. Margaret's 'face is vizard-like, unchanging,/Made impudent with use of evil deeds' according to York (I.iv.116–17), who goes on to characterize hers as a 'tiger's heart, wrapp'd in a woman's hide!' (I.iv.137) But the Lancastrians mark Richard as exceptional, unnatural, as a kind of challenge; Old Clifford makes the first reference to Richard's deformity in *Henry the Sixth, Part II*. Already this is in a context where the physical is read, by Richard's enemies at least, as a moral emblem;

> Hence, heap of wrath, foul indigested lump,
> As crooked in thy manners as thy shape!

(V.i.157–8)

Richard can either (as his family seem to) reject this, or he can adopt it and turn it against their enemies. Richard adopts monstrosity by making it, as his enemies have done in talking about him, his badge, his uniform. So it becomes pointless to separate off the psychological from the emblematic in reading Richard's body, and the personal history from larger histories – the familial, the national, the providential – in the reading of that emblem.

He accepts his singularity. His body has begun to make sense to him; as an emblem, but as monstrous, as an exception. We can return to Marlowe here. The depiction of Barabbas in *The Jew of Malta*, and of Edward II, creates a dynamic particularly challenging to a modern audience with a twentieth-century sense of the consequences and roots of anti-semitism and homophobia. These characters are stigmatized as outsiders, 'monsters' in a sense, but instead of asking for pity or understanding Marlowe presents them taking on the identity constructed for them, and outdoing their enemies' imaginations in a vengeful enactment of the role of murderous alien or unnatural king. Richard's deformity is read by his enemies as the outward sign of an inner nature. His identity is his enemies' gift, and, like Barabbas and Edward, he turns it against them. Richard chooses to be an expression of the forces that have 'shaped' him; if the 'heavens' have shaped the violent history of which he is a part, then he is the embodiment, the physical expression of that history, and here he decides to take on that identity, and to enact it on the largest scale open to him.

## HUMPING LADY ANNE

Most modern actors and directors bring with them some of the baggage of the realistic, psychological mode of acting developed in Europe and America over the eighteenth and nineteenth centuries, and formulated most powerfully by the Russian theoretician and director Konstantin Stanislavski.[13] Such actors are likely to conceive of character in terms which make an investigation of Richard's earlier career attractive. Of course, the same objections can be made to this imaginative linking of the three plays as a tale of coherent character and psychological change as can be made to the manufacturing out of them of a historical 'cycle'; rather more, in fact, as the psychology implied is more clearly anachronistic. Nonetheless it does not seem to me that we can be quite so sure of Shakespeare's conception of personality that we can reject readings stemming from such an approach out of hand. Antony Sher, in *The Year of the King* (1985), combines an account of his rehearsals for Richard with allusions to his own process of personal investigation through Freudian analysis.[14] The book is partly about what it is to be an outsider – a homosexual, a Jew, a white South African in Britain at a time before the end of apartheid. Sher's physical energy and charisma, combined with a Freudian/Stanislavskian approach to the preparation of the role, created a figure both sexually compelling and in himself sexually disturbed – misogynistic, with a grudge against his mother. In that twentieth-century acting tradition to which Sher belongs – introverted and personal in preparation, however extrovert in delivery – the actor requires a personal point of contact with the character. It is in the nature of the play that this is likely to remain private, especially when *Richard III* is performed on its own. Richard, in his 'own' play, is notably not introspective, not self-revealing, in the very extroversion of his address to the audience In a psychological reading, physical disability/deformity is on one level – a level that perhaps matters more to the actor than to the audience – the source of an understanding of the character's actions. Richard's sexuality, if one wants to think about it in modern terms, is complex and unclear. Richard has a will and energy that seem clearly libidinous, but his physical shape is a challenge to the libido – both his own and ours, the spectators.

That the figure of Richard had a kind of sexual significance from the beginning can be seen from John Manningham's anecdote of 1602:

> Upon a time when Burbage played Richard III there was a citizen grew so far in liking with him, that before she went from the play she appointed him to come that night unto her by the name of Richard III Shakespeare, overhearing their conclusion, went before, was entertained and at his game ere Burbage came. The message being brought that Richard III was at the door, Shakespeare caused return to be made that William the Conqueror was before Richard III.[15]

One could interpret Richard's sexiness as an aspect of fascination with the 'monstrous' and point to Dickens's Quilp in *The Old Curiosity Shop*, as a similar case, frightening and fascinating in the combination of energy (Richard's 'speed') with 'deformity'.[16] As Pauline Kael points out in a review of Daniel Day-Lewis's Oscar-winning performance in the film *My Left Foot*, the sexuality of the disabled figure is immediately present to the audience:

> At times, Day-Lewis's Christy uses his eyes to speak wicked thought, for him, as Olivier's Richard III did. They're flirts, these characters. As for the actors, when they're deformed they're free to be more themselves than ever.[17]

The way the performer must use his eyes creates an intensely erotic focus. And, as with Richard, Christy Brown, the figure Day-Lewis plays, exercises his own desire in a situation where he feels he is, inevitably, both looked at all the time, and, in any sense that would be important to him, overlooked. But it is surely also significant that a non-disabled performer, known from other roles to be strikingly handsome, is playing the role, and we as his public are seeing something different behind the performance of grotesque disability – disability only being describable as 'grotesque' when it is 'performed'.

Richard begins 'his own' play within the same rejection of courtship and love as marked by his self-defining speech in *Henry the Sixth, Part III*, but where there the dynamic is of the taking on, the learning to use, an individuating characterization imposed in hostility, in *Richard III* an already established identity is mobilized in ways that perhaps run away with the protagonist, get beyond his control. Within the wooing of Lady Anne, he discovers a kind of use for courtship; but that courtship is in a sense his undoing. One cannot find the physically identical figure in *King Henry the Sixth, Part III* 'sexy'. It is Anne who eroticizes the later Richard, and in doing so she gives him the means to extend and elaborate his persona. She does this by not taking him at face value:

> ANNE   I would I knew thy heart.
> RICH.   'Tis figur'd in my tongue.
> ANNE   I fear me both are false.
> RICH.   Then never was man true.
> ANNE   Well, well, put up your sword.
>
> (I.ii.196–9)

This lays the ground for a kind of double-bluff, which from now on becomes Richard's game in his relation to the other characters; his physical shape is an index to his psychological nature, in his self-presentation to us, the audience, but he tries to persuade other figures in the play to deny what, in the crudely negative reading of his body as emblem, had before seemed obvious to them. Maybe – or so he tempts them to think – he is something else, trapped within that body.

In thinking Richard's looks might hide something with a potential for herself, Anne reads erotically, projecting depths of meaning susceptible to and potentially rewarding her investigation. Anne gives Richard a new paradigm of identity. But at the same time, by rendering it relative, dependent on others' approval, she takes the possibility of personal identity away from him. Richard may feel himself to have acquired power at the outcome of this scene, but in the long term he has lost it. The figure who emerges at the end of *Henry the Sixth, Part III* was invulnerable, this is not. From now on he is a performer within the erotic theatre that Anne creates. A play of identity is of the essence of flirtation. This starts Richard on a game dangerous not only to others but to himself. While in *Henry the Sixth, Part III* we see him formed, in this play we see him pulled apart.

This dependence is very much part of the eroticism, perhaps its source. Winona Rider, Anne in the Pacino film, throws herself into the anger of the scene, but then manages a challengingly flirtatious throwaway delivery of her final 'since you teach me how to flatter you,/Imagine I have said farewell already.'

(I.ii.227–8)[18]. For all its medieval setting, Ian Holm's encounter with Janet Suzman's dizzy Chelsea babe of an Anne in *The Wars of the Roses* has an unmistakably sixties feel to it. In the television version the atmosphere of 'Swinging London' amorality is underlined here in his conspiratorially laddish look to the camera as Anne launches into her melodramatics.

But do Richard and Anne desire each other? This, as part of the larger question of their motivation, has been a recurrent and apparently irresolvable controversy in writing on the play.[19] Coleridge, for example, found the whole scene unbelievable.[20] It might make more sense to see the two characters colluding to create an erotic situation. In terms of their own individual situations this, for the moment at least, seems to open up possibilities, though in both their cases it signals an eventual defeat. As always, Richard's real relationship is to the audience. It is we who are flattered, wooed, our approval and amusement extorted; the actor has to seduce, or the play has no way of going forward.

The scene sets a trap both for her and for...can we call him her 'victim'? Anne is in modern parlance 'an ambulance chaser'. She talks herself into situations which she has no need to be in – there is no reason why she cannot simply leave the court and live a peaceful life in the country, but she seems to have to write herself into situations, however dangerous, that make her feel important. There is no reason for her to be the solitary mourner of Henry's corpse. Kristin Scott Thomas's performance in the McKellen/Loncraine film brings this out particularly well. The simple fact of transposing the play to a twentieth-century setting makes us aware that this woman cannot exist in a ritualistic vacuum. She needs to bring herself back into the court circle by what ever means are available, and as soon as possible. Scott Thomas's version of the role as a drug-abuser lays the ground for a genuine insight into the oddity and isolation of Anne's choices to parallel the sense of her masochistic exploration of the depths to which, in her world, it is possible to sink, as outlined by Jan Kott.[21] The scene in which Anne hazily recounts her story to the stony-faced group of the other women at an outdoor tea-party is one of the memorable moments of the film. Her relation to others is, in any version, a matter of the recounting of narrative – she writes herself, fatally, into the story, rendering herself, as a body, disposable. Her 'illness', which she predicts herself, is shocking in the very casualness with which Richard goes on to present it – it is purely a matter of report; words now have precedence over bodies. In the Lindsay/Moshinsky production, Anne was kept on stage, in Richard's grip, while he told us that 'I'll have her, but I will not keep her long'. She overheard from a doorway the news of her imminent demise. In the Lesser/Noble staging, Richard announced this news directly to Anne, who was sitting slumped on the throne next to him. Later in the scene she slipped to the floor, and crawled slowly and painfully off the stage, in a production which, perhaps to compensate for Lesser's mercurial presence and puckish looks, went to extremes in stressing his violence towards the women.

Marilyn French writes of Richard's contempt for women, in terms of a character that is 'masculine...unmitigated by any tinge of the feminine'. French is a pioneer of a feminist criticism which reinstates an interest in who is doing what to whom and why, and so frees the play from the previous academic emphasis on its relation to Tudor historiography and into the sexual arena in which most of its fascination for audiences has always lain.[22] This is not merely a matter of whether Richard himself is a misogynist; it takes us back into the psychosexual dynamic of the play as a whole, to the audience's reaction to it, and to the gendered ideologies that shape the aristocratic politics it depicts.

A comedy by the American playwright Neil Simon, *The Goodbye Girl,* has its actor-protagonist forced to play Richard as homosexual, a joke constructed within the stereotypically homophobic terms of the Broadway theatre of the 1970s. Here, *Richard III* provides the subtext of the modern romance, the sparring relationship, which the film version sets up between Richard Dreyfuss and Marsha Mason, playing the two semi-employed performers who are the lead characters. Their relationship, like those in the play, is based on territorial struggles, and has at its centre a wise child, Mason's daughter. The play was based on the experiences of Mason (then married to Neil Simon),[23] who, in 1979, played Anne in one of a sequence of productions of the play starring Michael Moriarty: 'psycho-sexually complex, a handsome emotional retard whom dramatic critics usually took to be homosexual'.[24] In the film the homosexual reading of Richard is presented as obviously ludicrous, and the performances both of the 'gay' director and of Dreyfuss as a gay Richard are stereotyped to an extent that gives some plausibility to the actor's protest in the film that 'Gay Liberation is going to hang me from Shakespeare's statue – by my genitalia!' He continues... 'I want my hump! I want my clubfoot!' The director's point has been that these are simply a metaphor for the situation of Richard, 'the queen who wants to be king' – 'it's society that makes him deformed'. Dreyfuss's character complains to the director 'lets not lose his motivation – he wants to hump lady Anne'. But is it that simple? One critic (Richard Burt) has recently celebrated the film as demonstrating 'a fundamental lack of heterosexual symbolic authority'.[25] So, by extension, the fictional 'director' in the film, and the real director of the film become (in the second case unwittingly) proto-queer theorists.

This scene is a powerfully sexual one, but its dynamic is about as 'straight' as Richard's back. There is nothing in it to suggest that he feels any particular attraction to Anne, or even that he takes a sexual pleasure, however perverse, in 'conquering' her. The sexual dynamic is Richard's discovery of his own desirability, and this 'crooked' self-eroticization, the deflection off the other of an image enticing to oneself, is the discovery (Shakespeare's and Richard's) which powers the rest of the play. In Britain at least, many of the most notable actors of the role have been 'out' homosexuals – Sir Ian McKellen and Antony Sher are the most notable recent examples – others out-ish. Still others have been presented in their repertoire of roles and/or in gossip as sexually ambiguous, from Colley Cibber in the eighteenth century through to Laurence Olivier in our own. The academic reader of the first draft of this volume argued with the remarks above apparently on the basis that so many English actors are gay; anyway the question is a matter of whether in a particular role such a fact, and such a public knowledge/ suspicion of that fact signifies. It did not in the case of say, John Gielgud's or Nigel Hawthorne's Lear; that it can seem to in the case of Sher's or McKellen's Richard – and, more to the point, that they themselves have made it so – might well tell us something about the role.

Richard presents a marriage to Anne as a strengthening of his claim to the throne:

> The readiest way to make the wench amends
> Is to become her husband, and her father:
> The which will I, not all so much for love
> As for another secret close intent,
> By marrying her which I must reach unto.

(I.i.155–9)

But it is not clear what the 'secret close intent' is. If it is political, it could be simply that Richard needs a queen in order to be king; it is a marriage in show, exploiting someone already made vulnerable, in order to participate in the flamboyantly heterosexual atmosphere of Edward's court. Or the 'intent' could be psychological, private to Richard – a revenge on women? A secret triumph? Whichever it is, it is not disclosed. The historical Anne was a wealthy heiress, and Richard, like most of his family, had lost a lot of money in the preceding wars.[26] This all deepens, rather than, as the character in *The Goodbye Girl* seems to hope, resolves the matter of Richard's motivation. Emrys Jones is surely right, in a moment crudely edited in *Looking for Richard* for an anti-academic belly-laugh (it follows one of Pacino's histrionically blokey collaborators making fun of the idea of scholarly authority), to say that as far as the play goes...he really doesn't know.

## THE MYTH OF THE HOLY CRIPPLE

At no point in the play are we invited to see Richard's deformity as a source of pathos. Sher identified the fallacy of the 'holy cripple', in itself a denial of the justifiable anger of the disabled, as a block on making sense of their plight.[27] The other most famous literary and theatrical hunchbacks, Victor Hugo's Quasimodo in *Notre Dame de Paris* and Triboulet, the jester, in his *Le Roi S'Amuse,* later the source of Verdi's *Rigoletto,* act as a kind of corrective to the tradition of Richard, a demonstration that the soul and the body do not necessarily correspond, and that the 'deformed' individual is trapped in a crisis of identity in their relation to the larger world. But within this play we are never invited to see Richard's abhorrent appearance as disguising a potential for good, or to identify in him a thwarted ability to make caring relationships (like that of Quasimodo to Esmeralda or Triboulet/Rigoletto to his daughter Blanche/Gilda), or to intuit a personality that may have been at least normal in different circumstances.

Where the French texts emphasize a contradiction between moral and physical being, in the English tradition Richard is elided into an unrespectable and vulgar enjoyment of the presence of monsters, a sympathy with the monstrous which has nothing to do with seeing it as misunderstood, everything with sharing in the rage and libidinous energy that the 'monster' unleashes. Quilp, in Dickens's, *The Old Curiosity Shop*, is the most vivid and complete of variations on this theme.[28] Dickens alludes to Shakespeare to the extent of locating Quilp's residence at Tower Hill, with a view of the Tower of London, a location that plays such a large part in the Shakespeare play. Like Shakespeare's Richard, Quilp is associated with the childish and the grotesque, and his energy and power are persistently sexual. But – and perhaps here he is closer to Shakespeare than the modern productions are – he is a monster and a spectacle rather than a psychologically explicable human being, explicable in normal terms at least. Like the play, the novel is disturbing simply because it extends, rather than seeks to correct, our received version of the human.

# 2

## Deformations of History

### 'AS THE FAME RUNNETH...'

While Thomas More did not invent the myth of Richard's deformity, his account elaborated it and fixed it in popular historical consciousness. There is no evidence contemporary with Richard to suggest disability. No existing portraits can be dated unquestionably from within Richard's lifetime, let alone be known to have been painted from life. In the earliest, which belonged to the Paston family, there is no hint of deformity, and Richard is placing a ring on the finger which at this time represented marriage, so the picture may well be designed to commemorate his marriage to Anne. The slightly later picture, the source of the most familiar image of the historical Richard, shows him fiddling with a ring on his little finger, which in the way images of the 'guilty' Richard have been read (the way in which we try to interpret the most trivial behaviour of those in the dock for major crimes) has been interpreted as nervousness, even guilt. X-rays made in preparation for the exhibition on Richard organized for the National Portrait Gallery by Pamela Tudor-Craig revealed that this image had been doctored in order to add in the requisite hump:

> The x-ray taken of this picture for the preparation of the catalogue revealed an alteration in the outline of the king's right shoulder; as originally drawn, it was lower than at present. The difference is enough to give that hint of deformity which is carried through in all versions of this type. The underlying layers of paint also show that the eye was first drawn in a less slit-like fashion. If panel dating allows, it is arguable that the picture in its original condition was of the time of Richard III. Alterations consistent with Tudor propaganda could have been made from any date from 1486 onwards.[1]

Yet another picture, showing Richard with a broken sword was altered with the opposite aim of regularizing Richard's looks when, in the seventeenth century, the counter-process of revisionary history had begun.[2]

More's physical description of Richard, quoted at the start of the previous chapter (p. 20), builds a structure of qualification around the apparently crude presentation of Richard as monster. His use there of negative forms – 'not untoothed', 'None evil captain was he in the war' – raises the spectre of a doubt which, in the case of the first idea, is qualified in verbal formulations that recur frequently in More – Richard's monstrous birth, is qualified further by '(as the fame runneth)..., whether men of hatred report above the truth, or else that nature changed her course...'. Horace Walpole, in his *Historic Doubts on the Life and Reign of King Richard the Third*, in 1768 one of the earliest attempts to argue against the accepted version, comments waspishly at one point that 'it is not sufficient ground for our belief, that an historian reports them with such a frivolous palliative as that phrase "as some say".'[3] Walpole's short book sold well. He describes his project as follows:

> It occurred to me some years ago, that the picture of Richard the Third, as drawn by historians, was a character formed by prejudice and invention. I did not take Shakespeare's tragedy for a genuine representation, but I did take the story of that reign for a tragedy of imagination. Many of the crimes imputed to Richard seemed improbable; and, what was stranger, contrary to his interest.[4]

Walpole's attitude is informed by an enlightenment, rationalist, contempt for the 'monkish chroniclers' of the medieval period. He lists Richard's seven 'crimes', the killings referred to in the play, 'to which may be added, as they are thrown into the list, his intended match with his own niece Elizabeth, the penance of Jane Shore, and his own personal deformities'.[5] Walpole is not, he says, 'going to write a vindication of him. All I mean to show is that, though he may have been as execrable as we are told he was, we have little or no reason to believe so'.

The sources of the play have a suspicious genealogy. More, writing one generation later than the events, was in touch with living witnesses, but by this same token he may be compromised by his relation to them. Josephine Tey's novel *The Daughter of*

*Time* (1951) is a detective fiction in which Inspector Alan Grant of Scotland Yard, finding himself bed-ridden and bored as a result of an accident incurred when chasing minor contemporary criminals, satisfies a need to exercise his mind by solving, with the help of a flamboyant actress friend and an earnest young American postgraduate student, the mystery of the murder of the princes. Tey makes much of More's early association with Archbishop Morton, the Bishop of Ely in this play, who joins Richmond, and was a supporter of the historical Henry VII. She ingeniously switches responsibility for the crime of murdering the princes in the Tower to Richmond, as the one with more to gain. In her account, Morton has set up More to do a whitewash job on Henry, and shift the blame onto Richard.[6] The novel is a concerned and witty worry at the relativity of history. It is conditioned, as were so many important productions of the play, by the experience of the 1939–45 war, and the suppression of information, the disinformation and the propaganda which conditioned that generation's experience of public events. The play, on the other hand, allows no room for doubt as to Richard's guilt. We witness this and the other killings Richard contrives in their planning and execution. His crimes here are simple, and knowable. As Alison Weir points out, More's acquaintance with Morton was in his early adolescence, and his relation to Henry was poor, to say the least of it; Henry imprisoned More's father and tried to fine More himself for not bowing to his will[7].

A generation later again, the chronicler Edward Hall uses More as one of his sources in a comprehensive and complicatedly organized account of the history of the civil wars, with an explicit programme of arguing the rightness and God-given inevitability of the uniting of the red rose and the white in the marriage of Richmond and Elizabeth. Hall's *The Union of the Two Noble and Illustrate Famelies of Lancastre and York* (1548) shapes More's narrative, with an emphasis invoked in the red rose/ white rose symbolism in Richmond's last speech. Holinshed's *Chronicles of England*, whose second edition of 1587 Shakespeare also used, draws in turn on Hall, while being more populist, less philosophical, arguably less 'official'.[8] So Shakespeare's interpretation of events has gone through a sequence of distorting lenses. Events and historical characters have been digested into fictions before he has encountered them. He seems to have no particular interest – as a twentieth-century writer or film-maker would have, however fraudulently – in claiming that he at last tells the truth. It is that layering of fictions of which popular history consists that interests him.

This awareness of rhetorical trickery, and of the relativity of historical report, brings Walpole close to the concerns and methods of a play whose narrative he seeks to cast doubt on. The play builds on this sense of history as relative in ways that undermine any too simple a reading of the version of events enacted in front of us. More has it both ways – fixing an image of the historical individual which still has currency today, while tipping the wink to a reader whom he flatters into sharing his sense that perhaps we are all too clever to actually swallow this. Theatre is different; this private contract of knowingness is unavailable to it, in that we are constantly, publicly, aware that our attention is being contested for by warring rhetorics exercised in our presence.

The weight of preceding history has to be felt in a performance of the play, and it is a weight that pulls most of the characters down. The reference back to a tangle of complex and often horrific events dramatized in those Shakespearean plays which deal with the precedent history creates a problem for director and audience. But we need to be aware of this weight, not necessarily in precisely detailed knowledge, but as the force of accumulated memory. The characters in *Richard III* discuss history a lot – or at least they continually present to each other competing versions of what has happened in their uneasily shared past. Two major possibilities in the interpretation of history are at issue here. Does history have a pattern, a plan, and if so, who can tell us what it is? And, is there such a thing as historical truth, and if there is, how can we know it? If we accept the second of these propositions, as most people do, at least up to a point, we have worries about the play. And those worries might have something to do with our response to the first point. We might want history to have a pattern – the characters in the play certainly do – but when they articulate their feelings on this point they are in situations of extreme emotional stress and demoralization – so they hold a discomforting mirror up to our need to find such a pattern, a mirror that might just show us back our own anxiety. Richmond, at the end of the play, claims that his victory is a providential outcome, but, to quote Mandy Rice-Davies, a player in a much later historical crisis (the Profumo scandal of the British sixties)' he would, wouldn't he'.[9]

I will return to this point at the very end of the book; it seems to draw together several strands of academic response to the play, in making crucial to academic assessment of the play what to most audiences seems like a merely formal closure, a tidying up of an open-endedly anarchic energy of action. We (as an audience) inevitably approach the play in a suspicious frame of mind, suspicious of the exaggeration of Richard's evil, and sceptical as to that moral pattern which the characters in the play, and many of its critics, ascribe to the events it depicts, and so, by extension, to historical process in itself. In this sense a sceptical response to the play as history is more than a cranky adherence to fact as such, or a worry about Tudor propaganda; it may be the recognition of an internal incoherence, and the play itself may draw our attention to this. The contemporary dramatist John Arden has spoken of Shakespeare's plays having a secret play within themselves, an inversion of the official overall argument that one might take the piece to be giving at a first superficial glance. There is enough in *Henry V*, for example, to allow us to read it as a reflection of the futility of conquest, the transience of glory, however nobly achieved.[10] If this is the case with *Richard III*, the secret play is a play of the fabrication of history, and this drama reflects on, in order to correct, distortion; the 'distortion' of the official propaganda of the story line that informs the play.

## 'MARGARET WAS A PROPHETESS', OR MAYBE NOT...

Many academic critics take it for granted that the play is providential in its account of history. This is to say that it follows an officially approved medieval and Renaissance theory of history in which providence, or in Christian terms, God, is the author of a pattern of which human beings are a part; their actions, whether they realize it or not, contribute to the grand and ultimately benign plan. This view can be traced back to

Tillyard and Campbell, and though the critical controversy seemed for a while to have been decided in favour of those who dispute this assumption, it has more recently returned in various different ideological contexts.[11] How far do we have to accept this to make sense of the play? Perhaps we should make a distinction between a fatalism that characters in extremis take on themselves, and a philosophy that underlies the play as a whole.

The agent of a sense of providence in the play herself compromises the idea of providence. Margaret, the exiled queen of *Henry VI*, is the play's chief witness and rememberer of a pattern that seems to be structured by fate. She turns up at the first court scene, talking to the audience or to herself, unseen by the other characters on stage. Historically Margaret never returned from her exile in France, an exile to which at the end of the play she returns. The play is careful not to literalize or explain her presence on stage; there is no plot reason for her to be there, and no physical journeying or means of transportation is invoked. She exists in the play out of time and space. Brian Cox, who played Buckingham in the Ian McKellen/Richard Eyre production at the RNT, asks:

> I still want to know why Queen Margaret is allowed to wander round the palace, I find it quite extraordinary. I had a theory that she might be hidden in a dumb-waiter that goes up and down, there are about three of them and she's actually hiding in the walls.[12]

This vagueness about the material situation of the character leaves the director and designer a free choice in designating the degree of decrepitude and insanity of the character – some Margarets have been sybil-like, almost dignified, others like June Watson (ESC), who, still in the remnants of her army commander's uniform, was both batty in herself and a frightening reminder of what has happened.

In this play, when taken alone, Margaret is more like a kind of ghost. In any case, her entrance must have been a surprising moment for the original audience, as it is ahistorical, not to be predicted from knowledge of the sources. Margaret is an echo from the past, an unwanted return of the events which the court characters, even or perhaps especially in peace-time, have to struggle to disentangle and accept.

*Enter old* QUEEN MARGARET.

ELIZ.  I had rather be a country servant maid,
Than a great queen, with this condition,
To be so baited, scorn'd, and stormed at:
Small joy have I in being England's queen.

MARG.  [*Aside*] And lessen'd be that small, God I beseech Him:
Thy honour, state, and seat is due to me.

RICH.  What, threat you me with telling of the King?
Tell him, and spare not: look what I have said
I will avouch't in presence of the King:
I dare adventure to be sent to th'Tower.
'Tis time to speak: my pains are quite forgot.

MARG.  [*Aside*] Out, devil! I do remember them too well:
Thou kill'dst my husband Henry in the Tower,
And Edward, my poor son, at Tewkesbury.

(I.iii.107–20)

Margaret in some sense represents history – if we see history as a process of repetition. Like Richard himself, but for different reasons and in different ways, she cannot let the apparent peace and accord of Edward's court stand undisturbed. Also like Richard, she can be read from a twentieth-century perspective as disturbed, traumatized by the events chronicled in the preceding plays. So perhaps she represents a form of anti-history – the treasuring and obsessive representation of trauma are the antidote to history if we see history as a way of moving forward.

Richard's characterization of Margaret as a witch – 'Foul wrinkled witch, what mak'st thou in my sight?' (I.iii.164) – has a topical relevance to the play's first audiences. In this play, the idea of witchcraft and the decayed or deformed body ('wrinkled') come together in a shifting of blame for Richard's deformity and, by extension, the moral deformity it represents. Just as witches were accused of malign attacks on the wellbeing of their social superiors (often male), so all women in the world of this play become potential victims of a witch-hunt that has at its root the deformed son's resentment of his mother; the malign witch is a parody, an inversion, of the nurturing mother.[13] We may remember that the narrative that Richard invents to account for his situation in *Henry the Sixth, Part III* is a tale of intrigue between two pagan goddesses, 'Love' and 'Nature', figured as venal court ladies; very much the terms in which the Richard of

44

*Richard III* characterizes an intrigue between Elizabeth and Jane Shore, as the fictional source of his deformity (III.iv.59–75).

The end of Elizabeth I's reign and the increasing likelihood that James VI of Scotland would become king created an official anxiety about witchcraft on both sides of the border. As well as malignancy, prophecy – especially prophecy of the exact timing of the queen's death – was at issue here.[14] Like Joan Puzel (historically Jeanne La Pucelle) in *King Henry the Sixth, Part I*, Margaret is threatening because she claims foreknowledge of historical events.[15] But, though characters at their demise tend to remember that 'Margaret was a prophetess', Richard realizes that her authority is easily subverted.

> MARG.
>
> .    .    .    .    .    .    .    .    .
>
> Thou loathed issue of thy father's loins,
> Thou rag of honour, thou detested –
> RICH.   Margaret!
> MARG.           Richard!
> RICH.                   Ha?
> MARG.                       I call thee not.
> RICH.   I cry thee mercy then, for I did think
>     That thou hadst call'd me all those bitter names.
> MARG.   Why so I did, but look'd for no reply.
>     O, let me make the period to my curse!
> RICH.   'Tis done by me, and ends in 'Margaret'.
> ELIZ.   Thus have you breath'd your curse against yourself.
>
> (I.iii.232-409)

Margaret may be partly sceptical of the cursing which she undertakes; she speaks not from a position of authority, but from one of uncontrollable emotional need.

> Can curses pierce the clouds and enter heaven?
> Why then, give way, dull clouds, to my quick curses:
> Though not by war, by surfeit die your King,
> As ours by murder, to make him a king.
>
> (I.iii.195–8)

That question could be genuine rather than simply rhetorical, and this is how some performers (Peggy Ashcroft, in *The Wars of the Roses*, for example) have taken it. The result is a curse in the more mundane sense of the word as, to use Alice Birney's characterization of it, a 'satiric catharsis'.[16]

As predictions, the 'prophecies' can be construed as common sense, the hard-won common sense of a woman who has lived through extremes of violence and unpredictable political change. It doesn't take much to realize that Edward is more likely to die, at this stage, from 'surfeit' than from war, nor is it hard to guess that the group of people in front of Margaret are unlikely to stay in accord. The characters she 'reads' are ones she knows well already – when faced with a stranger (the test of any clairvoyant) she gets him – Buckingham – exactly wrong.

> MARG.
> . . . . . . . .
> O Buckingham, take heed of yonder dog!
> Look when he fawns, he bites; and when he bites
> His venom tooth will rankle to the death.
> Have not to do with him; beware of him;
> Sin, death, and hell have set their marks on him,
> And all their ministers attend on him.
> RICH.  What doth she say, my lord of Buckingham?
> BUCK.  Nothing that I respect, my gracious lord.
>
> (I.iii.289–96)

Margaret is undoubtedly rhetorically powerful, perhaps to the extent that she convinces herself. But that the characters later believe that Margaret 'was a prophetess' is a token of their vulnerability – or evidence that the truth is obvious and banal.

Shakespeare leaves it open, as to whether magic and prophecy have any coercive power in the world the play presents to us. The prophetic dreams of Clarence and Stanley could equally well be read as common sense breaking through in the form of dreams, in a situation where common sense has to be repressed from the waking life if things are to be bearable. And it doesn't take much to realize that the holding of two separate councils, the thing that makes Stanley anxious (III.ii.11–12), is worrying if you have only been invited to one of the two.

## THE IMPORTANCE OF SCRIVENERS

The play is concerned with how we know history and what, when we think we know it, we actually know. The players in the aristocratic feud have a personal memory of what they have done to each other in the past, but there are characters outside that – the citizens, the scrivener, the young princes – who offer a meditation on the history that accumulates out of it. The scene at Bayard's Castle demonstrates Richard and Buckingham's manipulation of history through what in the twentieth century has come to be known as 'public relations'. Shakespeare introduces a character, the Scrivener, who has no function other than to draw our attention to this issue.

> Here is the indictment of the good Lord Hastings,
> Which in a set hand fairly is engross'd,
> That it may be today read o'er in Paul's.
> And mark how well the sequel hangs together:
> Eleven hours I have spent to write it over,
> For yesternight by Catesby was it sent me;
> The precedent was full as long a-doing
> And yet within these five hours Hastings liv'd,
> Untainted, unexamin'd, free, at liberty.
> Here's a good world the while! Who is so gross
> That cannot see this palpable device?
> Yet who's so bold but says he sees it not?
> Bad is the world, and all will come to naught
> When such ill-dealing must be seen in thought.

(III.vi.1–14)

In the Lindsay/Moshinsky production, which made intelligent use throughout of cutting and overlapping action to create continuity, the scrivener, or professional scribe, had been on stage throughout the preceding mayhem, calmly putting his document together. More is the ultimate source for this moment in the play:

> Now was this proclamation made within .ii. hours after that he was beheaded, and it was so curiously endited, and so fair written in parchment in so well a set hand, and therewith of it self so long a process, that every child might well perceive, that it was prepared before. For all the time between his death and the proclaiming could scant have sufficed unto the bare writing alone, all had it been but in paper and scribbled forth in haste at adventure. So that upon the proclaiming thereof, one that was school master of Paul's of chance standing by, and comparing the shortness of the time with the length of the matter, said unto them that stood about him here is a gay goodly cast, foul cast away for haste. And a merchant answered

him, it was written by prophecy...[17]

More's undercutting of Richard's proclamation bolsters up his own authority as the translation of verbal, person-to-person information into a written text. But why should we take More's text to be more authoritative than that which the scrivener or his equivalent have been employed to provide? His citation of the comments of anonymous bystanders gets him into an area in which the truth of his sources can neither be established nor challenged. The writing of Hastings's condemnation shows us how untrustworthy written record can be; indeed, the detective work of More's anonymous schoolmaster takes us closer to the speculation that lies behind books like Josephine Tey's, and the continuing interest in Richard of many amateur historians and internet users. Shakespeare's play makes a more clear-cut point. The very unconventionality of the scrivener as a dramatic character, and his irrelevance to the plot in any larger sense, gives a choric authority to a scene that offers a commentary to the play as a whole. It exposes the two things that make historical truth not only, as Wilde put it in *The Importance of Being Earnest*, 'never pure and rarely simple', but also in exceedingly short supply; the sheer easiness of falsifying record, and the terror and repression ('who's so bold but says he sees it not?') that silences objection. There is a scrivener behind every historical 'fact', a human agency which allows of the possibility of distortion or mistake. By putting him on stage, the play reminds us that that particular man has his own knowledge and opinion. It also creates a disclosure of that knowledge to us – theatre, in contrast to the private reading for which More's text was designed, creates a public illusion of privacy, in which characters like the scrivener, whom we never see again, tell us something which they simultaneously tell us cannot be told.

More, as we have seen, often uses a rhetorical construction like 'wise men', or 'men say', which instates the reader in a complicity with the narrator. When the play puts on stage a group of citizens to comment on events, the effect is somewhat different. No longer anonymous or abstract, these figures move towards a sort of shared knowledge whose nature is public; not the private deduction of the solitary reader to whom he addresses himself (a male, statesman-like, pan-European reader, particularly in the Latin version of More's text) but a public ground-swell of oral history and proverbial wisdom. More claims to reflect this, but of course we only have his word that he is doing so. The play presents the audience, specifically the London audience of its first performances, still just about in touch with the events of two generations or so ago, with a mirror to itself, and a challenge to its own memory, in contradiction of the official falsifiable, censorable modes of the written. On their way to a meeting with Richard, the citizens are anxiously trying to establish for themselves a history that makes sense:

> 3 CIT.   Woe to the land that's govern'd by a child.
> 2 CIT.   In him there is a hope of government,
> Which, in his nonage, council under him,
> And in his full and ripen'd years himself,
> No doubt shall then, and till then, govern well.
> 1 CIT.   So stood the state when Henry the Sixth
> Was crown'd in Paris but at nine months old.
> 3 CIT.   Stood the state so? No, no, good friends, God wot!
> For then this land was famously enrich'd
> With politic, grave counsel; then the King
> Had virtuous uncles to protect his Grace.
>
> .     .     .     .     .     .     .     .     .     .
>
> 2 CIT.   Truly, the hearts of men are full of fear:
> You cannot reason almost with a man
> That looks not heavily and full of dread.
> 3 CIT.   Before the days of change still is it so...
>
> (II iii.11–41)

This scene is seldom if ever performed. (A shortened version of it formed part of the Rodway/Hands RSC production, and the Lindsay/Moshinsky version invented a prophetic nun, to deliver some of the salient lines to an attendant priest at the beginning of the 'sanctuary' scene.) It is, however, an important part of the play's argument about what constitutes historical memory, as the end of the scene shows the citizens – not quite 'ordinary people' (though Hands had them as a mixed group of men and women who were also responsible for moving furniture on and off), more the rich and influential citizens of the city of London summoned to receive Richard's official version of events. The play ends up operating through a broader sense of what history is written in and on than simply the matter of the trustworthiness of written evidence and the partiality of published interpretation. These events have as their markers not only the written, but a lively oral tradition, and the buildings of London itself. The play constantly refers to the physical sites of events, in order to trigger memories in the original audience which were after all only two or three generations away from them[18]. The McKellen/Loncraine film plays witty computer-assisted variations on this, in using currently empty buildings from the late nineteenth and earlier twentieth century to stand in for the historical monuments mentioned in the play – St Pancras hotel, for example, next to the British Library, becomes the royal palace. This, and the rest of the visualization of the piece, locates the play in a set of confused images of twentieth-century English culture. The effect is parallel to that of Michael Bogdanov's ESC history cycle, and of Derek Jarman's film of Marlowe's *Edward II* (1990). In all these cases the accoutrements of English establishment style trigger audience reminiscence and response to locate and to some extent account for the action of the play within the self-mystifying, self-elaborating structures of English tradition. Jarman and Bogdanov filter their presentation of the historical material through ritualized forms of upper-class behaviour still current, and still effective in that ambiguous area between the social and the formally political in which decision-making in England seems to occur. There is something rotten in the state of England – a monster like Richard, who in the McKellen/Loncraine film stands in for the fascist potential of the twentieth-century English aristocracy.

Olivier's pre-war stage version, and audience reaction to it, was influenced more immediately by the rise of Hitler; Olivier said that it created a tension in the performance, by virtue of the fact that evil was no longer a laughing matter, no more just the material of melodrama.[19] The film of the play that he both directed and starred in is post-war; the performance is embedded just as much as its opposite image, his film of *Henry V*, in the politics and mood of the time. The expressionist use of shadow and colour in itself links back to pre-Hitler German cinema, and Olivier's sensual, even tacky exploitation of lurid technicolour and post-expressionist, Disneyish visual effects – he based his nose on Disney's Big Bad Wolf – create a powerful sense of historical and libidinous nightmare.[20] Perhaps an implication in the politics of the time speaks more eloquently when unwilled – the McKellen/Loncraine film, read this way, speaks rather depressingly of the 'end of history', a very fin-de-siècle refusal to even try to make sense of things. The effect is to lose all historical referent; in a flattening of the cinematic image into two-dimensional visual styling and on evocations of twentieth-century history (what if 'Edward', whose liaison with what in the film is an American Elizabeth, Annette Benning, parallels that of the reputedly Hitler-friendly Edward VIII with the American Wallis Simpson, had been reinstated on the throne from which he abdicated because of her – as Hitler is said to have promised him. What if Oswald Mosley, the British Fascist leader, had been Edward's discontented brother?). All of this seems more playful than illuminating. History, in becoming the subject of the film, becomes trapped in the medium of the computer-generated visual image, all so easily manipulable, like Richard's early portraits, and the visceral confrontational excitement of the play, the sense it gives of an all-too-immediate encounter with the violence of events, is lost.[21]

The play as written uses a cityscape whose features are in view of the theatre itself as a concrete form of memory. London, particularly the area around the Tower, to which the play most persistently returns, has history made present in its monuments. The Tower has an ominous effect on Prince Edward when he sees it:

> PRINCE.   I do not like the Tower, of any place.
>     Did Julius Caesar build that place, my lord?
> BUCK.   He did, my gracious lord, begin that place,
>     Which since, succeeding ages have re-edified.
> PRINCE.   Is it upon record, or else reported
>     Successively from age to age, he built it?
> BUCK.   Upon record, my gracious lord.
> PRINCE.   But say, my lord, it were not register'd,
>     Methinks the truth should live from age to age,
>     As 'twere retail'd to all posterity,
>     Even to the general all-ending day.

(III.i.68–78)

Caesar was famously the chronicler of his own victories.[22] Edward goes on to cheer himself up from his fearful (and accurate) reading of the Tower as an agent of oppression, by seeing it in a larger perspective, where it represents the possibilities of Caesar-like greatness for himself (III.i.78–94). The physical remains of history are presented as the materials of an ongoing heroic story in which the prince wishes to play a part, though we know his only role will be as the victim of his uncle's ambitions.

The domain of this kind of 'knowledge' is the theatre, a new kind of building on the London cityscape and a kind of machine of communal memory, the medium of a history both public and unofficial. The Elizabethan theatres would, as the recent reconstruction of the Globe has shown, be permanent-looking – imitations of the grandeur that was Rome – but, in being built on a windy location out of lathe and wood, have the exciting precarious and warmly inclusive feel of a ship, setting out on dangerous waters. Theatre of necessity creates a different kind of history from that created by the written word, in that its medium is the sense of a moment shared by audience and performers; we are not privately looking over a text, as More's or Hall's envisaged readers are. We are offered the illusion of a kind of time-travel, a trip back to the events to which the texts allude. There is plenty of evidence that the Elizabethans found this to be the most exciting and valuable function that theatre has.[23] Theatre in this context is a kind of institutionalized communal memory, given concrete form in its buildings and in the performances they contain. The play is constructed to heighten this sense for its original audience.

Like others of the Shakespeare history plays, and Marlowe's *Edward II*, there are many scenes where what cannot be known – the concealed murderous decisions which are the lynch-pins of Shakespeare's dramatizations of history – are made visible to us in a way that, in the very nature of the dramatized circumstances of the actions involved, stresses that we are being made witness to a secret act, whose historical truth is actually unverifiable. That is precisely what is exciting about what we see. History is an access to the forbidden. The play has a memorably violent atmosphere but – and perhaps this is why the tension and the sense of fear build so seamlessly for the audience – it shows no act of violence on stage, until the killing of Richard. (Several directors, including Hands, have had Hastings killed on stage, but this seems to disrupt an effect carefully calculated by the dramatist.) Poor Prince Edward is a victim of history, however we read his fate. He is not to be, like his admired Caesar, the chronicler of his own deeds, but to go to an unrecorded fate – a too familiar phenomenon of that twentieth century experience of history which, in Western Europe after Hitler, and in Eastern Europe after Stalin, has made the play so much less easy to take lightly.[24]

In recent English theatre much of the power of this sense of the play has been lost, and replaced by the differently powerful sense of it as the study of a troubled charismatic individual. The design of the McKellen/Loncraine film, like details in other recent productions – the bare 'interrogator's' light bulbs in the Russell Beale/Mendes RSC production, the black hoods on the condemned Dorset and Rivers in the Troughton/Pimlott – rest on the dangerous line between visual quotation and unaffecting cliché. The Bogdanov production makes nightmarish satirical capital of its collage of newsreel memories, but it is significant that the most powerful visualization is John Bury's for the Barton and Hall *The Wars of the Roses*, a Berliner Ensemble – influenced concept where the alienating strangeness of a medieval world is constructed in metal and coarse fabrics, realized into crude heavy shapes – this is both medieval and modern, almost industrial; a mid-century vision of the inhuman historical machine. This production and the ESC's apart, the play seems, in a post-war British context, less about history than it is about theatrical history.

# 3

## Plays and Players

The beginning of Act III, scene v, has in the folio version and in editions based on it (like Hammond's Arden edition, which I use here) a stage direction which draws our attention to the self-conscious theatricality of the action:

> *Enter* RICHARD, *and* BUCKINGHAM, *in rotten armour, marvellous ill-favoured.*

In this scene Richard and Buckingham use theatre in order to establish Richard's claim to the throne, by putting on an act to persuade, impress and – probably more importantly – intimidate the Lord Mayor of London and a group of citizens. Although the 'rotten armour' is not immediately obvious in its relevance, we get a strong sense that Richard and Buckingham are dressing up and adopting, almost playfully, the resources of theatre. It's a charade, wobbling on from moment to moment with more chance of going wrong than most productions (and editions based largely on the Folio) allow. The 'rotten armour' is a detail from More which the Quartos leave out, probably because it is never alluded to in the dialogue, and so seems puzzling at a first reading. It is there to suggest that they are about to be attacked, and have only been able to throw together this improvised and inadequate mode of defence. It belongs with stage directions like Elizabeth's entrance 'with hair about her ears' (II.ii.33) as pointing to a visual, iconic style of staging and an extrovert and physical acting style. But the show is only on the road once the mayor and the citizens enter.

> BUCK.   But what, is Catesby gone?
> RICH.   He is, and see, he brings the Mayor along.

*Enter the* [LORD] MAYOR and CATESBY

BUCK.  Lord Mayor –
RICH.  Look to the draw-bridge there!
BUCK.  Hark, a drum!
RICH.  Catesby, o'erlook the walls!
BUCK.  Lord Mayor, the reason we have sent –
RICH.  Look back! Defend thee, here are enemies!
BUCK.  God and our innocence defend and guard us!

    *Enter* LOVEL *and* RADCLIFFE, *with Hastings's head*

RICH.  Be patient, they are friends: Ratcliffe and Lovell.

(III.v.11–21)

In the context of this fraudulent manipulation of events, politics
is theatre, and the drama is more than simply a medium of
representing history; theatre is the means by which history
happens. This again is derived from More, but there the idea is
inflected rather differently:

> With this there was a great shout, crying 'King Richard King
> Richard'. And then the lords went up to the King (for so was he from
> that time called) and the people departed, talking diversely of the
> matter every man as his fantasy gave him. But much they talked and
> marvelled of the manner of this dealing, that the matter was on both
> parts made so strange, as though neither had ever communed with
> other thereof before, when that themselves well whist there was no
> man so dull that heard them, but he perceived well enough, that ail
> the matter was made between them. Howbeit some excused that
> again, and said all must be done in good order though. And men
> must sometime for the manner sake not be a known what they
> know...in a stage play all the people know right well, that he that
> playeth the Sultan is percase a souter [i.e., a shoemaker]. Yet if one
> should can so little good, to show out of season what acquaintance
> he hath with him, and call him by his own name while he standeth
> in his majesty, one of his tormentors might hap to break his head,
> and worthy for marring of the play. And so they said that these
> matters be kings' games, as it were stage plays, and for the more part
> played on scaffolds. In which poor men be but the lookers on. And
> they that wise be, will meddle no farther. For they that sometime
> step up and play with them, when they cannot play their parts, they
> disorder the play and do themselves no good...[1]

More's citizens seem to be describing something both dangerous and empty, aimed at them but meaningless to them. Richard
needs their assent, but their granting of it is cautious, formal.

55

They spot easily that what is going on is wrong, but that insight produces a careful, considered distancing of themselves from events, rather than protest or intervention. The political event, according to More, depends on the spectators knowing their right relation to it, and their own survival depends on their arriving at the right kind and the right degree of complicity.

Theatre here is an emblem of vanity, of the emptiness of shows of power. The 'two bishops' who turn up 'aloft' with Richard in the later Bayard's Castle scene (III.vii.93) must surely be an obvious fake that the citizens can see through; there are, after all, only so many bishops about at any one time, and identity of these is unspecified. Performances have often played them as soldiers or thugs in transparent disguise. Like the 'marvellous' 'rotten armour', this suggests that the play, at its mid-point presents roles and uniforms as empty of meaning and all too easily adopted by those who aim at power. This is comic, but it is also frightening, in that it makes visible the power-lessness of the citizens. Like the court councillors in the scene of Hastings's arrest, they are unable to object to something they know is false. But at the same time Shakespeare, like More, is fascinated by the potential for creating a politically powerful self through show, through a use of the means of theatre. There is no theatre in More's Utopia, the fantasy of a perfectly functioning state, which he describes in a Latin treatise of the same name;[2] it wouldn't be necessary, as power relations there are all clear and universally accepted. In a real and distinctly non-Utopian medieval or Tudor London, as both More and Shakespeare are aware, power is maintained by representation, of a kind that is either overtly theatrical, or for which theatre provides the most accessible analogy.

When we watch a play, we are conscious of our presence in the theatre, a very different political situation from the discreetly private wisdom of the humanist scholar, as the Elizabethan city authorities were well aware, and as their worries about assemblies in public theatre at times of political ferment show.[3] That awareness has several levels. On a metaphorical level, we become in a way performers; we are cast as posterity, even at the end, maybe as a judging God. But we are also the judged; by this time we should have been recruited to some extent to an empathy with Richard. In rehearsals for the

Sher/Alexander production, Richard was encouraged to address his audience in the first scene as 'trainee Richards', a point that parallels Freud's reading of the play's power for its audience. But then again the on-stage action may well put us under threat.[4] A good production should make us feel that we are in the same time zone as the on-stage audience – the citizens, the courtiers or whoever. To this extent the play moves out of its medieval context all too scarily easily. A nineteenth-century or earlier twentieth-century audience may read the play as a Renaissance response to the dark ages, mapping it on a model of progress of which the very existence of a liberal academic readership was itself a part: but in the post-war context, Richard has re-emerged as a highly twentieth century play – not least in its sense of the role played in political events by the image, by performance, by propaganda.

## HOW STUPID ARE THE CITIZENS?

The reactions of the mayor and the citizens in the scene with which we began are not entirely clear; has Richard fooled them? Modern productions have tended to play the citizens as stupid; Mendes for the RSC had the mayor as a solid burgher with a comical Northern accent – nonsensical as a medieval lord mayor of London, and as a cheap laugh too much a token of the company's metropolitan bias to go down well on the Northern tour on which I saw the production. Hands had a gaggle of frightened, gauche, black-bearded citizens, who gibbered with fear when the bloody stump of Hastings's head was waved in their faces, and who adopted accents more suitable to playing Fagin in *Oliver*. The McKellen/Loncraine film presents the scene with the citizens as Richard's propaganda coup. This seems not only to work against the scene as written, but to be incoherent in itself. (Brian Cox, in his production diary, makes a similar point about the McKellen/Eyre stage version).[5] Apart from a few shots of people running around with flags at the beginning of the Bayard's Castle scene, there is no preparation for the massed Nuremburg rally that in the film returns Richard's final salute; the single shot in which we are shown this moment is disorientating – it is, like so much of the film, a quote from another film (this time from Leni Riefenstahl's Nazi celebration of Hitler, *Triumph of the Will* )

This sequence differs between Quartos and Folio, which suggests that an ambiguity as to how far the citizens are convinced, and if so why, existed from the early performances of the play. In the Quartos, the mayor enters on his own, and Catesby enters with the head of Hastings before Richard and Buckingham have had the chance to establish, however unconvincingly, that there is a plot to attack them. I quote from Kristian Schmidt's edition of the first Quarto.

> *Enter Maior*
>
> Glo.  Here comes the Maior.
> Buc.  Let me alone to entertaine him. Lo: Maior,
> Glo.  Looke to the drawbridge there.
> Bvc.  The reason we haue sent for you.
> Glo.  Catesby ouerlooke the wars.
> Buck.  Harke, I heare a drumme.
> Glo.  Looke backe, defend thee, here are enemies.
> Buc.  God and our innocence defend us. Enter Catesby
> Glo.  O, O, be quiet, it is Catesby. with Hast. head.
> Cat.  Here is the head of that ignoble traitor...

This is much more broadly farcical than in the Folio; there Buckingham and Richard's plot looks more plausible, and more of Richard's minions are around to make the arrival of the head more impressive. In the Quartos Richard and Buckingham have to improvise maniacally and not quite convincingly – Catesby has got the timing of his entrance seriously wrong.

Two things are at issue here – how stupid are the citizens? And how far was the city associated with Edward IV, who established many of its institutions, and his city-born mistress Jane Shore, who, as with so many royal mistresses, at least until the era of Princess Diana and Camilla Parker-Bowles, was a genuinely popular figure? Olivier's film makes the point wittily, by contrasting Elizabeth's cool demeanour and mechanical hand-wave from her carriage as she leaves Edward's coronation – her style is very much that of the house of Windsor – with the hearty popular greeting given to a sexy Jane Shore as she is carried in her chair through the crowds at the end of the same event. Unlike, Heywood's play on the same story, called *Edward IV*, or Dekker's *Shoemaker's Holiday*, where Edward returns to the city from France as victorious king and *deus ex machina*, Shakespeare represents Edward in purely negative terms, as a prematurely ageing bon viveur. (John Wood, in the McKellen/ Loncraine film, is very effective in this role), and minimizes Jane, whom an Elizabethan audience would probably expect to see. Shakespeare is less interested in reflecting city interests than were many of his dramatist colleagues, so perhaps the tendency in modern-day Shakespearean performance to present all the non-aristocratic characters but for the 'loveable rogues' of the canon as stupid and/or funny does have some basis in the writer's own attitudes. But there are other possibilities in presenting the play theatrically. The mayor and citizens are in a position where wary withdrawal is an intelligent reaction – we have no sense that they either believe or disbelieve what Richard and Buckingham claim; they have the sense to see that they are in a kind of play; indeed their initial response suggests that it's a kind of flop. We might go back here to the 'rotten armour'. While in More the point of this is that Richard and Buckingham have dashed on against a sudden threat, armed in whatever they could find, the visual effect in the play, without this explanation, is that they are a miserably tacky, basically clown-like act, a parody of the martial or the regal. The whole sequence eerily encodes the emptiness of the titles Richard and Buckingham aspire to, as an emblem of vanity which their performance makes visible to us without their observing its relevance to themselves The point of Richard here is that he entirely lacks a Hitlerian charisma. There is less of a fascistic euphoria, more of a kind of Soviet bloc irony to the citizens' reaction; nobody is bowled over, everyone knows that this is a trap that they have to negotiate their way around as adeptly as they can.

The traditional interpretation of the play, both in stage performance and in literary criticism, has tended to exaggerate the extent of Richard's triumphs. Outside the inner circle of the court, Richard's actions make very little difference to the country and its people; we might contrast him here with *Macbeth*, where it is made clear both in the action and in the powerful structure of metaphor in the play that what happens in the court affects the whole nation. *Richard III* does not allow its central figure – except perhaps retrospectively, when Richmond demonizes him in his final speech – this kind of mystical, quasi-natural force (III.v.85–93).

## HOW STUPID IS RICHARD?

As Julie Hankey has shown, Cibber's version held the stage because it tried both to account for Richard's actions, and to present him at the end as heroic; it allows one to see him as a powerful mind gone to the bad.[6] Though this version of the text is no longer current, the reading of the role that it promoted is. Certain scenes get pulled into the (unexamined) notion of a rhetorically powered Ricardian rollercoaster.

The improvised play of Guildhall and Bayard's Castle scenes signals the beginning of Richard's decline, by making him the property of another, Buckingham. Buckingham's power has depended on his not having been involved in the previous dynastic shenanigans; he seems like a free agent. We might go back here to the opening of the scene, his private rehearsal with his collaborator, and, at this point at least, his friend. Buckingham and Richard convey nervousness and bravado in roughly equal measure.

> RICH. Come, cousin, canst thou quake and change thy colour,
> Murder thy breath in middle of a word,
> And then again begin, and stop again,
> As if thou wert distraught and mad with terror?
> BUCK. Tut, I can counterfeit the deep tragedian,
> Speak, and look back, and pry on every side,
> Tremble and start at wagging of a straw,
> Intending deep suspicion. Ghastly looks
> Are at my service like enforced smiles,
> And both are ready in their offices
> At any time to grace my stratagems.

(III.v.1–11)

In the idea of 'counterfeiting the deep tragedian' Buckingham claims he can counterfeit a counterfeiter; this might create a double level of deceit, or it could be that the two levels of counterfeiting cancel each other out and leave us with something that has a kind of truth; the revelation of the tawdriness of their performance renders it a truthful parody of the grotesquerie of ambition. There are messages here for Richard that at this stage he is unable to hear.

RICH. Touch'd you the bastardy of Edward's children?
BUCK. I did...

· · · · · · · · ·

                          his own bastardy,
As being got, your father then in France,
And his resemblance, being not like the Duke.
Withal I did infer your lineaments –
Being the right idea of your father,
Both in your form and nobleness of mind

                                          (Ill.vii.4–14)

This is going a little too far. Buckingham has already given out a signal which Richard would be wise to heed:

        Doubt not, my lord: I'll play the orator
        As if the golden fee for which I plead
        Were for myself; and so, my lord, adieu.

                                          (III.v.94–6)

Is he acting 'for myself', with a longer-term objective? His public wooing of Richard ends with a threat – or just another double bluff...how is Richard to know? Buckingham is flamboyantly histrionic here – 'Zounds!' – in the style of his pre-mayor rehearsal. But how should Richard respond to 'we will plant some other in the throne'?

        Yet know, whe'er you accept our suit or no,
        Your brother's son shall never reign our king,
        But we will plant some other in the throne
        To the disgrace and downfall of your House;
        And with this resolution here we leave you.
        Come, citizens; zounds, I'll entreat no more.
RICH.   O, do not swear, my lord of Buckingham!
*Exeunt [Buckingham, Lord Mayor, and Citizens].*

                                 (III.vii.213–19)

Shakespeare's history plays often explore the idea of the king as player, and academic criticism has often explored this illuminatingly, especially in relation to the idea of 'The King's two bodies': that is, the medieval and Tudor doctrine of the double nature of the individual ordained king or queen, as both vulnerably human and divinely sanctioned in a way that makes them outside normal human laws.[7] There is a tension, a vulnerability about even the most outwardly confident of

Shakespeare's rulers. Only the incompetent and defeated Richard II is absolutely sure of the sanctified basis of his title. Usurpers, tyrants, those in possession of unsanctified power, gained through dubious means, like Richard and Macbeth, seem hollow both to us and to themselves. As Macbeth puts it:

> Life's but a walking shadow, a poor player,
> That struts and frets his hour upon the stage,
> And then is heard no more. It is a tale
> Told by an idiot, full of sound and fury,
> Signifying nothing.
>
> (V.v.24–8)

Macbeth's metaphor for life – 'the poor player' – comes out of his sense of himself as impersonating rather than truly being the king. The fact that an actor, is at the moment of articulating this, occupying a stage in front of us enables the very act of performance to become a metaphor that, in the very moment of performance, unites Macbeth's consciousness of his position and the consciousness of the spectator. The Bayard Castle and Guildhall scenes of this play seem to put Richard in the same position, but through our realization of the situation he is in, rather than in any ability of his own to reflect on it. Until the eve of his death, Richard very deliberately cuts himself off from reflection. In this context theatre itself becomes a moralized emblem, an emblem of the emptiness of human life. The player, the king and death – and the fool, the 'antic' (Macbeth's 'idiot') who combines aspects of all three, and in whose identity all three participate – are, for Shakespeare symbolically continuous with each other. The player here has something in common with the skull as memento mori[8] (as in the Holbein picture) of the hollow crown, the seat of death as Shakespeare presents it in *Richard II*:

> For God's sake let us sit upon the ground,
> And tell sad stories of the death of kings:
>
>   .   .   .   .   .   .   .   .   .
>         ... within the hollow crown
> That rounds the mortal temples of a king
> Keeps Death his court, and there the antic sits,
> Scoffing his state and grinning at his pomp ...
>
> (III.ii.155–63 )

The Rodway/Hands production ended with Richard and all the characters who had appeared as ghosts led in a dance of death by a skeleton dressed in black armour; the death figure gave Richard his death blow, then the assembled ghosts, like the characters in Agatha Christie's *Murder on the Orient Express*, all put the knife in on their own behalf.

## THE FORMAL VICE INIQUITY

Richard has already drawn attention himself to a theatrical tradition, that of the medieval morality and mystery plays, in which he could be placed, as a devil figure or a 'vice':

> Thus, like the formal Vice, Iniquity,
> I moralize two meanings in one word.

(III.i.82–3)

He has become aware here, in the middle of offering an aside to the audience to undercut the precocious Prince Edward's meditations on history, and recovering from being nearly overheard, of the possibilities of playing with meaning and manipulating the audience. This is the keynote, for many academic critics, of his self-presentation, and a pointer towards the generic richness of the play.[9] A vice is not necessarily the embodiment of evil – the word comes not from 'vice' as sin, but from the word for 'mask', as in 'visor'.[10] Richard's mother makes the same connection:

> Ah, that Deceit should steal such gentle shape
> And with a virtuous vizor hide deep Vice!

(II.ii.27–8)

The vice plays with identity and with verbal meaning, offering others a risky route towards the fulfilment of their own desires. This aside scarcely gives us a clue to the whole character. It tells of a momentary enjoyment in controlling something that in the long term is out of his control; it's unusual, and fun, for Richard to feel like a vice, to have that sense of covert dominance and irresponsibility. To make this clearer we could compare him to Edmund in *King Lear* or Aaron in *Titus Andronicus*, who have the vice's crucial combination of rhetorical control, often in direct address to the audience, with the ability to influence and change the direction of other characters' desires, the power to lead them on to commit violent actions, from which the vice himself stands back. Like many male Shakespeare characters, we see Richard in the bulk of the play in a situation where he is out of character – Hamlet isn't normally that miserable, Othello used to be impressive, Coriolanus never tried to think before. Richard was always the used, never the user. Until, for the first half at least, in this play.

A more consistently analogous figure from medieval drama is the Antichrist, a once familiar character in the Mystery cycles,[11] though now only one play concerned with this character, the Chester play, survives. John Rous, in one of the earliest chronicle accounts of Richard's reign, makes the same connection.[12]

Antichrist imitates and parodies the actions of Christ, rather as Richard can be seen to imitate and parody true kingship, and he acquires total power, the empery of the world, through trickery and show. But his reign is put to a stop by the emergence of true prophets – it was always only an interim, signalling the return of Christ to earth in judgement, at the end of the world. Richard towards the end of the play is interrupted in his ceremonial progress by a group of women, as Christ was by his mother and her companions on the way to Calvary.[13] Richard refers to himself as 'the Lord's anointed' (IV.iv.151), while the duchess continues the reference by swearing 'by the Holy Rood' (IV.iv.166). Like Richard, Antichrist doesn't recognize that he is a victim, not a victor, and that Christ is a victim who eventually triumphs. The setting of the Sher/Alexander production aimed to take the play back to the medieval mysteries. It was a detailed reproduction of a cathedral nave, based on Worcester Cathedral, with Richard and Richmond's tents looking like the mouths of Hell and Heaven, respectively.[14] The effect was more gothic, tomb-ridden; this was, significantly, a cleaned-up cathedral, 'restored' in Victorian style, with none of the colour and bustle of a medieval or Elizabethan equivalent. A basically naturalistic acting and directorial style overrode any suggestion of early and pre-Tudor drama. The effect was more of a 'gothic' fantasy of the middle ages, of the kind produced for Kean's Drury Lane production,[15] than of the carnivalesque and messy, the simultaneously pious and carnal middle ages, such as gave rise to the Antichrist plays. Our sense of Richard as actor,

CODLIN, SHORT AND COMPANY.

Illustration 5  *The Old Curiosity Shop*, from original illlustration by Phiz

65

like our sense of Antichrist, isn't very different from a sense of him as a puppet. Of all the Shakespearean roles, he is most easily reducible to a doll, a violent marionette. Dickens, in *The Old Curiosity Shop*, introduces the Punch and Judy man, as the helper but also the eventual betrayer of Nell and her Grandfather in their flight from Quilp.[16] Mr Punch is a violent hunchback puppet, derived from the Pulchinello of the *commedia dell'arte*, and possibly taking on himself some of the aspects of Richard (who may of course, given the earlier origins of the *commedia* tradition, have something about him of Pulchinello). Punch fights violently with Judy, his wife, threatens their baby, is in bad relation to the law, and generally provides the same spectacle of manic libidinous energy as Richard does. In popular tradition Mr Punch and hunchback Dick merge, as Dickens was well aware. Theatricality fulfils a variety of functions for Richard, but local political gains are overshadowed by a sense of theatre as the impermanent, a signal, in the long term, less of power than of powerlessness.

# 4

# Women and Children

## 'WOE TO THAT LAND THAT'S GOVERNED BY A CHILD'

Shaw, reviewing Irving's performance of the 1880s gave as a reason for the popularity of the play 'the world being yet little better than a mischievous school boy'. James Agate, in the 1920s, echoed the comment in calling the play a 'boy's play – for one boy to write and another to see.'[1] For these commentators there is something immature about a taste for *Richard III*, something immature about the play itself. But the suggestion that the play belongs to childhood has a resonance that goes beyond its pejorative context here. That a play that centres on the murder of children should be seen as childish takes us into complex aspects of its celebrity. A child's enjoyment of the play would have more to do with Richard's destructive energy than with the precocity and 'innocence' of the princes. In the nineteenth century the play was often performed by children; Julie Hankey records a performance by 'the two Bateman sisters, Kate and Ellen, who were then six and eight years old, as Richard and Richmond: "a nuisance by no means proportioned to the size of its perpetrators", wrote Henry Morley sourly.'[2] Though the third citizen's rather ponderous citation of proverbial, biblical,[3] wisdom – 'Woe to that land that's govern'd by a child' (II.iii.11) – is in literal terms a reference to Prince Edward, it can be extended, as it was, according to Norman Rodway, in the rehearsals for the Hands production, to Richard himself.

The child who seems most directly childlike, Clarence's son, is later dismissed by Richard as simple, and so no threat (the historical Henry VII/Richmond thought differently, and had him, as the nearest to the crown but for himself, imprisoned and eventually executed). This child questions adult behaviour, rather than joining in with it; it is his directness, his lack of flirtatiousness, which marks him as 'simple' in the performance-orientated world of the play. Though the boy is able to ask direct questions about the problem of disguise and deceit, his 'innocence' makes him incapable of accepting the answer he is given;

> BOY   Good grandam, tell us, is our father dead?
> DUCH.   No, boy.
>
> .   .   .   .   .   .   .
>
> BOY   Why do you look on us, and shake your head,
>    And call us orphans, wretches, castaways,
>    If that our noble father were alive?
> DUCH.   My pretty cousins, you mistake me both:
>    I do lament the sickness of the King,
>    As loath to lose him; not your father's death:
>    It were lost sorrow to wail one that's lost.
> BOY   Then you conclude, my grandam, he is dead:
>
> .   .   .   .   .   .
>
>            ...my good uncle Gloucester
>    Told me the King, provok'd to't by the Queen,
>    Devis'd impeachments to imprison him;
>    And when my uncle told me so, he wept,
>    And pitied me, and kindly kissed my cheek;
>    Bade me rely on him as on my father,
>    And he would love me dearly as a child.
>
>                                   (II.ii.1–26)

The princes, on the other hand, seek to 'join in' with the adult games of power. They place themselves in tales from history (like that of Caesar's building the Tower), steps in their curtailed education. They perform as a kind of double act for an on-stage audience all of whom have a different design on them, a different kind of knowledge, different experiences. The princes are supposed to be 'innocent' – that is the point of their performance – but they pick up on a sense of danger from their on-stage audience that inflects their act.

> YORK.   I pray you, uncle, give me this dagger.
> RICH.   My dagger, little cousin? With all my heart.
> PRINCE.   A beggar, brother?
>
> .   .   .   .   .   .
>
> RICH.   A greater gift than that I'll give my cousin.
> YORK.   A greater gift? O, that's the sword to it.

RICH.  Ay, gentle cousin, were it light enough.

.      .      .      .      .      .      .

It is too heavy for your Grace to wear.
YORK.  I weigh it lightly, were it heavier.
RICH.  What, would you have my weapon, little lord?
YORK.  I would, that I might thank you as you call me.
RICH.  How?
YORK.  Little.
PRINCE.  My lord of York will still be cross in talk;

.      .      .      .      .      .      .

YORK .      .      .      .      .      .

Uncle, my brother mocks both you and me:
Because that I am little, like an ape,
He thinks that you should bear me on your shoulders!

                                    (III. i.110–31).

Productions- including Rodway/Hands, Howard/Hands, McKellen/Loncraine – had York on that last line leap on Richard's shoulders – who then whirled around, maddened by pain and suddenly stung into violence, presumably by the sensitivity of his hump. But even before that the scene is a particularly tense one for the boy actors. Richard's 'A dagger, little cousin? With all my heart' has an obvious overtone of threat, comically immediate to an audience; it catches us in the familiar double bind of complicity with Richard – who has not thus tired of a precocious child? – and shock at so blatant a signal of what we already know will happen. York's then asking for the sword dramatizes the distinction between childhood and the adulthood to which he will be inducted when he is knighted and entitled to carry a sword. Richard's 'would you have my weapon?' suggests that his masculinity is threatened – the children are reducing him to a childlike level, as they demand that the symbols of his masculine status be passed over to him. Sher refers to the 'ape' idea as a 'taunt', but if it is so it is unconscious on the boy's part. It may not be tactful, but in all this the children are, in a friendly way, perceiving Richard as another child. The scene gives Richard a chance to show his childlikeness, which Sher did in playing the 'ape' to make the boys laugh.[4] The princes resemble Anne as victims in an uneasy complicity with their fates; they play with Richard, entering into a performance with him, but like Anne they cannot know how the contract implied in this will play itself out. The innocence of

69

the princes is constructed in adult response to them, a process that reaches a rather queasy climax in the narration of the princes' murder. In life, the children perform childishness, in a variety of contexts determined by the needs of the adults around them. In death they are more completely, because mutely, images of innocence.

It may not be immediately obvious why Richard, and not the men who actually do the killing, is the 'monster' of the princes' murder. The difference is that the murderers' motivations are financial, their behaviour professional, and so to that extent we accept them as adult. In adulthood you have a conscience, but you also have a sense of money, of the material world, which allows you to override it, if you can bring yourself to. Then you can have the luxury of remorse: for one of the murderers a luxury you pay for; for the other, one that for financial reasons he decides to forego:

> Take thou the fee, and tell him what I say,
> For I repent me that the Duke is slain. [*Exit*]
> 1 M.   So do not I: go, coward as thou art.

> (I.iv.267–9)

Richard shows a childlike lack of interest in moral consequence. He is, to that extent, innocent. If Clarence's children are one kind of child, the princes another, Richard is another again. It is something childish in us that draws us to Richard. He calls himself a child, but uses the idea within its associations of innocence and harmlessness – this only draws our attention to the other aspect of the childlike at issue in his behaviour, an unstoppable destructive energy, which the princes have been educated to repress, but which, to our delight (and envy) Richard has managed to keep intact and smuggle into the adult world.

## RICHARD KILLS THE CHILD WITHIN

Richard presents his energy to us as having its source in envy and its aim as appropriation of things – like Anne and the crown – which (childishly) he both does not really want and cannot use when once he gets them. If we take this play separately from the *Henry VI* plays our sense of Richard's motivation comes more

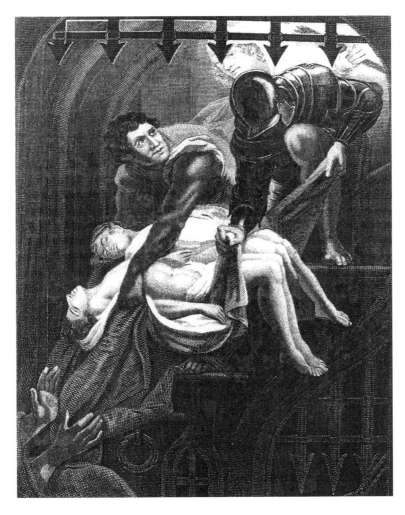

Illustration 6   James Northcote, *The Deposition of the Princes*

nakedly from childish appetites whose consequences we observe, but which we cannot securely criticize, as the play has the power to make us empathize with them. It comes, to that extent, from within ourselves, as Freud realized.[5] But the accumulation of communal and personal memory is an adult characteristic and pulls us, as the audience of 'cycle' presentations of the plays, in a different direction from our childish empathy with naughty Richard. The crucial difference lies in the kind of rapport with the audience which the later play creates. In the earlier, we are disturbingly close up to a damaged and dangerous personality – we are not in complicity with him, he does not 'entertain' us, as the later figure does, as our host at a murderous party. In the later play taken on its own, historical memory is less a motive than a means, an artillery activated rhetorically in struggles between characters motivated and energized by the more primal and childlike urges. But if we have seen the plays as a sequence we have witnessed the killing of a child, Rutland, Richard's brother. We have seen the killing of Richard's father, and we have heard Richard's reaction to the event.

To try to trace Richard's psychological development through the earlier plays may be, as I have already suggested, to import into them both a twentieth-century psychology and a twentieth-century sense of narrative form. But the reading we get is remarkably coherent; it may be in scholarly terms a fiction, a collage of historically discrete texts, but the resulting 'new' text is suggestive of an imaginative interest on Shakespeare's part in the links between criminality and family.

In *Henry the Sixth, Part III*, Richard insists on listening to the tale of his father's death at Margaret and young Clifford's hands in detail – 'Say how he died, for I will hear it all' (II.i.49) – and his reaction is to internalize his reactions;

> I cannot weep; for all my body's moisture
> Scarce serves to quench my furnace-burning heart;
> Nor can my tongue unload my heart's great burthen.
>
> .   .   .   .   .   .   .   .
>
> To weep is to make less the depth of grief...
>
> (II.i.79–85)

Richard's grief in the earlier play at his father's death, and his shock at the death of his youngest brother, Rutland, are intense and genuine; the logic of his path towards expunging any sense of the family from his internal economy and becoming, at the apex of his villainous career, a child-killer himself, could be explained in modern terms as a form of 'denial', a flight from trauma, and a remaking of himself. Now he is armoured within a defiantly individual and challengingly 'monstrous' persona. Our play doesn't resist this reading. Antony Sher, though he could not be bothered to read the *Henry VI* plays, watched the BBC television version, and was excited to see York played by a powerful actor, Bernard Hill, whom he had worked with in a production of the play at the Liverpool Everyman in 1973. In that production, directed by Alan Dossor, and conceived as the grotesque play of absurd figures trapped in a kind of circus cage, Jonathan Pryce was Richard, Sher was Buckingham and Hill played a sequence of small roles. Sher describes his excitement at seeing, in the television version, the family background of his character, the loss of a loved strong father, unfolding in front of him.[6] The speech where Richard recalls the killing of his father to Margaret is powerful, and one of the few passages expository of previous events to survive into the Quartos, but, unless we have seen the event enacted, we are unlikely to respond to these lines:

> The curse my noble father laid on thee
> When thou didst crown his warlike brows with paper,
> And with thy scorns drew'st rivers from his eyes,
> And then to dry them, gav'st the Duke a clout
> Steep'd in the faultless blood of pretty Rutland –
> His curses then, from bitterness of soul
> Denounc'd against thee, are all fall'n upon thee;
> And God, not we, hath plagu'd thy bloody deed.

(I.iii.174–81)

The effect of this trauma on Richard is now inscrutable. The play begins from a fixed and armoured image of one whose past has made him what he is, but in an erasure and denial of whatever in that past has made him vulnerable. He tells the story with a sense of its effect on the hearer, and, while a post-Stanislavskian actor might well want to dig into these references as the source of a motivation, for an audience at this point the focus is on Margaret (as, in the earlier trading of violent historical narratives, it had been on Anne), and unless that audience

73

already knows the earlier play, the moment is likely simply to blur into the welter of remembered violence, of accusation and counter-accusation, which creates a sense of chaos and imminent instability in the court scenes. An Elizabethan audience would know the story, whether or not they had seen the other play, but one can assume that they would be less likely to look for motivation of this kind. But even if we do not pick up on the historical detail, we realize that this narrative is, as far as Richard is concerned, centred firmly on the troublesome child within.

In this frankly anachronistic, but theatrically appealing reading of the three plays as a developing psychological history, Richard's mutation into a child-killer is signalled by a kind of denial of the facts of childhood and family, and of the obligations they ordinarily impose, a denial that allows him to define himself as entirely independent. Thus, the killing of Rutland can be seen to lie behind the killing of the princes.

> RIC. Dar'st thou resolve to kill a friend of mine?
> TYR. Please you; but I had rather kill two enemies.
> RIC. Why then thou hast it; two deep enemies,
> Foes to my rest, and my sweet sleep's disturbers,
> Are they that I would have thee deal upon.
> Tyrrel, I mean those bastards in the Tower.
>
> (IV.ii.68–74)

The characters Richard killed in the earlier plays were adult enemies; here he calls the princes' 'enemies', but they are only enemies of his egotistically defined ambition. He has moved from a narrative of dynastic conflict, in which he is held in place by family loyalty, to a narrative in which family no longer exists, and individual will is all.

The logic of this makes the structure of revenge of which the other characters in the play obsessively talk seem, by contrast, adult, human, sane. Their behaviour is like that of the various professional murderers; it involves the showing of a kind of balance sheet of crimes for which one can hold oneself or hold others accountable. To look for Richard's motive, we have to look into a murkier psychic economy, one that has nothing to do with even a pretence at moral book-keeping. Richard's destructiveness is all to do with appetite and impulse. 'Business first, pleasure arterwards', Sam Weller says in Dickens's *Pickwick Papers* 'as King Richard the Third said wen he stabbed the t'other king in the Tower, afore he smothered the babbies'.[7] (Weller, of course, like anybody else before Irving's production of 1875,[8] would have seen the play on the Cibber version, where King Henry is murdered on stage). The play at this climactic moment presents a crime that an amoral innocent commits on innocents.

## RICHARD'S MUM

The idea of childishness, the complexities of our response to it, is used to map Richard's relation to the other characters, and so his career. The two major figures here are his mother, the Duchess of York, and the Duke of Buckingham. Neither are present in the previous play. The York family there is presented as close, functional and all male. Where Richard's brothers and father are consistently affectionate to him, his mother is consistently hostile. Her presence is, like Margaret's, significant precisely because she has no direct relevance to the plot; she is there to be Richard's mum. Further, her role has no dynastic or political function, so she comes to represent mothering in itself. Sher was shocked at the first rehearsal where he met the actress to play his mother – she looked so like his own.[9]

The duchess functions as one of a quartet of women who are defined in relation to childbearing and marriage – Margaret who has lost her only child, Elizabeth whose energies are focused on not losing all of hers, and Anne, trapped in a marriage enigmatically both sexual and non-sexual. In this context the duchess is a kind of *über*-mother; she constantly draws attention to her womb and her breasts, and relates herself to the earth; she is near to death, her fecundity, in producing Richard, having become the inverse of itself – she describes her womb, in a phrase that brings to mind the death of the princes as 'the bed of death'(IV.i.53). In a way, she becomes equivalent to the Tower, as Elizabeth sees it:

> Pity, you ancient stones, those tender babes
> Whom envy hath immur'd within your walls –
> Rough cradle for such little pretty ones,

Rude ragged nurse, old sullen playfellow
For tender princes, use my babies well.
So foolish sorrow bids your stones farewell.

(IV.i.98–103)

This speech is not presented in the Quartos, presumably because it adds nothing to the narrative at this awkward late stage in the play. Modern productions always include it, as it adds a commentary on the web of associations set up in the play so far, on history and on the place of women and children in it. The prince, we may remember, is both frightened of the Tower, and fascinated by it as a marker of a history he has been brought up to see in relation to himself. The Tower becomes a cruel substitute for Elizabeth's womb. As a substitute mother – a nurse, but a flinty barren one – it is continuous with the duchess's age and her rejection of Richard, who, given the prolonged and difficult pregnancy, must have made her feel as if she was both imprisoned and imprisoning. The birthing reference may be there also in the 'deliverance' of Hastings from the Tower in I.i, by Jane's intercession; she is another witchy pseudo-mother.

In the play, Jane – silent, invisible – is the repository of Richard's and Buckingham's misogyny. Historically, Jane was the go-between for Hastings and Elizabeth, while the queen was in sanctuary, in the formulation of an ill-fated plot of escape which determined his downfall. The very fact that she had been the mistress of Elizabeth's husband may well have fitted her for this role, as less likely to be suspected of Elizabeth's confidence. But Richard seems historically, as well as in the play, to have chosen to represent this alliance as evidence of sorcery.[10] In the Rodway/Hands production, Richard had a joke withered arm, with bloody tendons attached, that came off in Hastings's grasp, after Jane had been accused of bewitching it. The 'deformity' for which she is blamed is one for which a mother might tend to blame herself. So in this reading he is inventing a fiction about Jane (everyone on stage knows his arm has always been 'withered', they just don't dare say so) which dramatizes his feelings about the mother who has rejected him.

This rejection can be used to provide another psychological clue to Richard, and this is how it was for Sher.[11] Lord Byron, who was himself 'deformed' (with a club foot) and very conscious of it, and on very bad terms with his mother, has as a persistent motif in his own plays the rejection of a flawed son by an unyielding mother, most flamboyantly at the beginning of his play *The Deformed Transformed*. 'Out, hunchback!' is the first line.[12] (The mother is called, of all things, Bertha.) Byron wrote in his journal after seeing Kean as Richard, 'he is a soul! Life – Nature – truth without exaggeration or diminution. Kemble's Hamlet is perfect; – but Hamlet is not Nature. Richard is a man; and Kean is Richard.' References to the play run through his letters and journals.[13] These fleeting but vivid reminiscences of the stage productions of Kean, and Cooke, whom Byron also admired, and their persistent surfacing as he wrestles with his own sense of self as ambitious, appetitive, deformed and unable to work out what he wanted from women is evidence of what a fascinating icon of masculinity these performances made out of Richard for a generation of Romantic theatre-goers, and of their emphasis on Richard's proto-Romantic individualism, the energy of a flawed but compelling anti-hero.

The sexual and familial contexts which define Richard stress motherhood as the origin of the individual and as a source of both power and vulnerability for the women in the play. Richard's twisted 'nature', his inhuman origin, is articulated by their presence. But, however powerful they may be in terms of what they represent or possess, they are, like the citizens, outside the official account and their voices are overruled. In More's account, the persuasive language of the archbishop overrides the disconsolate Elizabeth's instincts.

> The Queen her self sat alone a-low on the rushes all desolate and dismayed, whom the Archbishop comforted in the best manner he could, showing her that he trusted the matter was nothing so sore as she took it for ... [14]

The play creates a ritualized language, based on repetition and an address out of the immediate situation to 'heaven' or posterity, which gives the women a voice that simultaneously speaks of their silence in the face of power and allows them to challenge that power by foregrounding their identities as mothers and wives (rather than, in Margaret's case, her identity as general and ruler), as in our century 'the mothers of the disappeared' have challenged oppressive South American regimes. And, like their twentieth-century equivalents, the royal widows draw on the role of women in the Christian passion story to place their protest within a politics larger than the simply temporal.

'Why should calamity be full of words?' asks the duchess (IV.iv.126), a challenging moment for the actress, in that by this time the audience might well be feeling the same. She responds to Elizabeth's answer – 'they ease the heart' – with a gruesomely physical pun;

> If so, then be not tongue-tied; go with me,
> And in the breath of bitter words let's smother
> My damned son that thy two sweet sons smother'd.
>
> (IV.iv.131–4)

The physicality of her reference to smothering is a continuation of the idea of the power of the women's own breath, in forming damning words. Richard's trumpets and drums by means of superior martial and/or regal noise aim to 'smother' the voice of a mother who can be seen as wishing death on her own child. This also pulls together a web of references surrounding the killing of the princes. The idea of the crime sends Buckingham out of the king's presence to take 'breath' – 'Give me some little breath, some pause, dear lord,/Before I positively speak in this' (IV.ii.24–5) – its commission renders the murderers silent, and as we shall see, the 'smother ' idea is invoked again; it takes us into the idea of the 'unspeakable' – not just the crime itself but the psychological process that lies behind it.

## BUCKINGHAM'S CHILD

Buckingham's value to Richard is precisely that he is outside the precedent history. Margaret, as we have seen, miscalculates in appealing to him for sympathy, and his negative response to her advertises an enticing independence to the audience and to Richard. It would seem to be at this moment that Richard marks him out, not quite as an equivalent, rather as one truly independent, in a way that Richard can only aspire to be. The more Richard proclaims his independence, the more he draws our attention to his entanglement in a family history that is both public and painfully interior to him. Buckingham has no history, is no one's child – he truly is 'himself alone'. Norman Rodway, in interview, spoke of Richard as 'in love' with Buckingham, a love that springs from the support Buckingham gives to a figure otherwise rejected and at a loss in Edward's new world of peace. The powerful relationship between Rodway and Ian Richardson, as Buckingham, was the core of that production. But, like Margaret, Buckingham can be a victim of a production which focuses too exclusively on Richard. An earlier twentieth-century reinstatement of his importance – Ralph Richardson's performance in the Olivier film is a reminder that the role has in the past often been cast with an actor of equal status to the player of Richard – seems to have fallen away in the wake of the Sher/Alexander production, where Buckingham (Malcolm Storry) was understated to the point of disappearing. Sher's account of the on-stage accident that curtailed his performance as the Fool in *Lear*, the accident which lead to the rebuilding of his physique and movement style which became essential to his conception of Richard, is more suggestive of the relationship between the two characters than anything seen on stage (at least by the present author):

> Crawled into the wings. A crowd of stage-managers had gathered. 'Tony, what's the matter?' 'Don't know, can't stand up.' 'Are you in pain?' 'Don't know, don't know what's going on.' The next entrance was from under the stage, down several flights of stairs. Mal Storry (Kent) picked me up in his arms and carried me like a child...[15]

Richard, in the first court scene, says 'I am too childish-foolish for this world', presenting himself as 'soft and pitiful', an ambiguous characterization of childhood; full of pity towards others, innocent, well-meaning, good – or maybe an object of pity, because powerless, vulnerable. Buckingham can exploit the 'childish-foolish' side of Richard in a way that turns him back, not to innocence, but to his fear of vulnerability.

The play demands a balance between these two figures – equally good powerful actors, with a certain rapport. The McKellen/Eyre production was designed to tour with a production of *King Lear*, starring Brian Cox, directed by Deborah Warner. Cox played Buckingham to McKellen's Richard, McKellen, Kent to Cox's Lear. While this must have seemed a good idea in theory, the practice of rehearsing the two plays at the same time, especially given the directors' very different working methods, created some strain, and for Cox, at least, frustration. (McKellen has not recorded his views on performing Kent.)

> Basically there's one part, and it's Richard...Buckingham is especially evasive; he's a man who seems to talk a lot but say very little, an empty man. My friend Oliver Cotton, who played him at the RSC last year, gave me a tip; the man is godless, has lost his faith. I can well believe it, there is something hollow about Buckingham.[16]

Cox, developing the role, and perhaps feeding his own frustrations into it, decides that Buckingham is 'bored' and that he decides to promote Richard, the least likely candidate, out of a sense of perversity, to cheer himself up. Something similar was successfully conveyed by David Yelland in the Lindsay/Moshinsky performances, who played the role with the dry reserved manner of the able but uncaring. This was sometimes funny sometimes menacing, and always a telling foil to Lindsay's charismatic but emotionally retarded Richard. Which of them is the other's puppet? Who is ventriloquizing whom? A review of John Wood's National Theatre performance of Richard refers disparagingly to a 'Morecambe and Wise' sense of humour, and Julie Hankey records a review of an early twentieth-century Buckingham which complained that he 'pushed Richard about the stage' as if they were a music hall double-act.[17] Surely this is apposite to the play. Richard and Buckingham have the on-stage rapport and the hints of emotional tension, of unresolved rivalries and entrapping dependency, that make for the most powerful comic duos.

Buckingham comes across as the most intelligent and free character in the play, and so the one we are most likely to connect with, if the actor is capable of taking the opportunity. When he fails to give instantaneous support to Richard's wish to commit the play's central taboo act, the childish killing of children, Richard draws the distinction between himself and Buckingham in terms of an opposition of childhood to adulthood. In the scene with the citizens, Buckingham to Richard was as director to actor (which can be like parent to child). There, in his offer to 'plant some other in the throne' (III.vii.215), the parent is threatening to withdraw his love. As Buckingham goes on to do again, this time with fatal results for himself. It is not clear whether Buckingham is playing an ill-judged game with Richard, or whether he has a genuine revulsion from the idea of killing the princes – and whether, if he feels such revulsion he returns because he is able to overcome it. When he comes back, Buckingham tests Richard by asking him to fulfil his promise of 'Th'earldom of Hereford', but in the interim the plans for the murder have been made, and Buckingham has become redundant. Richard decides to place his confidences elsewhere:

> I will converse with iron-witted fools
> And unrespective boys; none are for me
> That look into me with considerate eyes.
> High-reaching Buckingham grows circumspect. –

(IV.ii.28–31)

The ability to reflect, to look into oneself, and so to make a complex set of choices in relation to other people – to be 'deep' and 'witty'- is the scariness of adults. Adults can talk, as Richard suspects Buckingham does, over the child's head. And adults have something called conscience. This is not in itself a moral quality, it is a kind of mental capacity, conveyed through the 'considerate eyes' that Richard, like a nervous animal, cannot bear to confront. This is the immediate trigger to the arrangement of the murder. Buckingham has rejected Richard, by claiming the need to think – he perfectly probably intends to agree to the killing. It is this pause for thought which troubles Richard, and moves him to assert himself in unthinking conscience-defying action. If conscience is a definingly adult capacity, Richard does not become an adult until the night before he dies.

### I LIKE YOU, LADS

Richard's real equal – or the equal to his imaginative sense of self as a guiltlessly naughty child – is the character he addresses at the end of the sequence quoted in the last section, the moment of Buckingham's exit from his coronation:

K. RICH.  Boy!

PAGE.  My lord?

K. RICH.  Know'st thou not any whom corrupting gold
    Will tempt unto a close exploit of death?

PAGE.  I know a discontented gentleman,
    Whose humble means match not his haughty spirit;
Gold were as good as twenty orators,
    And will, no doubt, tempt him to anything.

K. RICH.  What is his name?

PAGE.                          His name, my lord, is Tyrrel.

K. RICH.  I partly know the man: go call him hither.

[*Exit Page*]

(IV.ii.32–41)

This is the whole of the page's role. He is normally cut in modern performances (not in the Sher/Alexander, where he was polishing Richard's shoes, a more stageable version of More's account, where he is supervising Richard on the 'close stool', or chamber pot).[18] This is a pity, as he provides a further section of the spectrum of childhood that the play offers – an innocently (if you like) amoral child who neither cares about nor particularly enjoys his role in the destruction of two other children.

> ...he said unto a secret page of his: Ah whom shall a man trust? Those that I have brought up my self, those that I had weaned would most surely serve me, even those fail me, and at my commandment will do nothing for me. Sir quoth his page there lieth one on your pallet without, that I dare well say to do your grace pleasure, the thing were right hard that he would refuse, meaning this by sir James Tyrell...upon this page's words King Richard arose...and came out into the pallet chamber...on which he found in bed Sir James and Sir Thomas Tyrell, of person like and brethren of blood, but nothing of kin in conditions.[19]

The page's appearance in this play is a carefully contrived summary of a more important figure in an earlier anonymous play, *The True Tragedy of Richard the Third*, a play whose exact relation to the Shakespeare has never been satisfactorily resolved.

In *The True Tragedy*, the page not only finds Tyrel for Richard, but narrates the story of the murder; in this and his other interventions he (rather than Richard) acts as the vice figure. In the Shakespeare play the page's simple amoral presence reminds us that Richard's can have the directness of the child no more than he can have the independence of the 'formal Vice, Iniquity' (III.i.82).

In Shakespeare, it is Tyrrel who tells the story of the princes' murder.

> The tyrannous and bloody act is done;
> The most arch deed of piteous massacre
> That ever yet this land was guilty of.
> Dighton and Forrest, whom I did suborn
> To do this piece of ruthless butchery –
> Albeit they were flesh'd villains, bloody dogs –
> Melted with tenderness and mild compassion,
> Wept like two children in their death's sad story.
> 'O, thus', quoth Dighton, 'lay the gentle babes';
> 'Thus, thus', quoth Forrest, 'girdling one another
> Within their alabaster innocent arms;
> Their lips were four red roses on a stalk,
> And in their summer beauty kiss'd each other.
>
> (IV.iii.1–13)

This is an awkward speech for a modern audience, as is Olivier's technicolour visualization of it. 'The most arch deed of piteous massacre/That ever yet this land was guilty of' feels like an unsustainable overstatement, which the piling on of pathetic detail does nothing to compensate for. But the point is not so much to move us as to demonstrate how the murderers are moved; they become as children, weeping in contradiction of Richard's characterization of himself, that 'Tear-falling pity dwells not in this eye' (IV.ii.65). In Christian terms this is a prelude to their salvation. The princes become a fixed, cold ('alabaster') icon of sacrificed innocence. 'O, thus ... Thus, thus' gives Tyrrel the cue to hold out his arms, to convey the murderers' imitation of the children they have killed. The murderers' gesture – in embracing each other – would be comic if we were to see it, but as related it forms part of a pattern of ideas which suggests that the killers are saved by, in a sense, becoming their victims. The starting point of all this may well be More's description of Tyrrel sharing a bed with his virtuous brother. Another pattern, which I have anticipated in talking about the Duchess of York's puns on 'smother', emerges later in the speech:

TYREL                               ...'We smothered
The most replenished sweet work of Nature,
That from the prime creation e'er she fram'd.'
Hence both are gone with conscience and remorse.
They could not speak...

(IV.iii.17–20 )

The murderers' cutting off of the princes' breath has rendered
them silent themselves.

'The prime creation' is in contrast to Richard's tales of
nature's cheating deformation of his body. The princes
represent a lost perfection, with overtones of Christ. This
moment and images of it were the starting point of Boydell's
Shakespeare Gallery, a money-making project, whose wider
cultural *raison d'être* was to import into the visual arts in Britain
the genre of 'history painting' or painting on narrative themes,
which was felt to lie behind the pre-eminence of the European
old masters; English painting had portrait and landscape, and
was developing a genre of narrative domestic subjects, but
lacked the stimulation of big dramatic themes, just as it had lost
the catholic tradition of religious painting.[20] The picture of the
burial of the bodies is modelled on Caravaggio's *The Entombment
of Christ*. The princes' bodies are naked, the state in which,
according to More's account, they were shown to Tyrrel after the
murder, the state in which Richard's body, historically, was
displayed after his death at Bosworth.

Depictions of the princes were the most successful and
popular images in Boydell's gallery.[21] Their attraction is more
complex than mere pathos; the play's repellently elaborate
description of the princes' passive 'innocence' resonates not
only in patterns of 'smothered' voices and unshed tears which
come to dominate the remainder of the play, but in a cultural
matrix of imperilled childhood which Boydell lucratively fixed,
and which survived through the nineteenth century as a
troubling legacy to our own.

Richard needs to deny adulthood in order to operate as the
'monster' that seems the only logical way to be, if he is to be
Richard. His address to the killers of Clarence gives a further
clue to the way he configures the distinction between adult and
child;

RICH.　But sirs, be sudden in the execution,
　　　　Withal obdurate: do not hear him plead;
　　　　For Clarence is well-spoken, and perhaps
　　　　May move your hearts to pity, if you mark him.
2 M.　Tut, tut, my lord: we will not stand to prate.
　　　　Talkers are no good doers; be assur'd:
　　　　We go to use our hands, and not our tongues.
RICH.　Your eyes drop millstones, when fools' eyes fall tears.
　　　　I like you, lads: about your business straight.
　　　　Go, go, dispatch.

(I.iii.346–55)

Clarence's ability to use language – historically he was famed for his eloquence – is, again, something that Richard is frightened of. But Richard misreads the 'lads' on one other issue. Both sets of murderers, Clarence's, whom we see, and the princes', whose reactions are only reported, develop the power of conscience, the power of introspection. Richard may deny, or even be afraid of 'tears', but the murderers of the children learn to weep, and that suggests a lesson Richard is yet to learn.

# 5

# Mirrors and Shadows

## 'UNFELT IMAGINATION'

Mirroring is a dominant idea in the play, from Richard's sequence of soliloquies in the first act onwards. There they chart a growing self-confidence. At the start he is, by his own account, 'nor made to court an amorous looking-glass' (I.i.15). In the idea that the looking-glass is itself 'amorous', there is a narcissistic conflation of the imaginary lady and his own reflection; the lady is there to reflect him, but it is himself whom he courts, to woo his likeness into a liking of himself. Anne fulfils this function to the extent that purchasing an actual full-length glass – a large financial outlay in Shakespeare's time, let alone in the middle ages[1] – becomes a plausible fantasy:

> I do mistake my person all this while!
> Upon my life, she finds – although I cannot –
> Myself to be a marvellous proper man.
> I'll be at charges for a looking-glass,
> And entertain a score or two of tailors
> To study fashions to adorn my body...

(I.ii.257–62)

For Cibber this isn't quite extravagant enough; his 'I'll have my Chambers lin'd with Looking-Glass'[2] takes one back to the 'fops' and dandies of eighteenth-century comedy, the roles in which he made his name.[3]

'Mirroring' structures the play dramatically. After its mid-point, which is also its most self-referentially histrionic – Richard's performance to the mayor and citizens – events repeat and earlier scenes are echoed. The difference is that while the first half of the play showed Richard on an upward trajectory, the emphasis in the second is on his loss of control; this is the downward part of the arc of his career. The princes' murderers are appalled by what they have done; Clarence's had not been; Margaret's second appearance is gloatingly triumphant, where her first was pathetic, and Buckingham is no longer a reliable ally. And Elizabeth, as we shall see, seems to escape where Anne succumbed.

Richard's end is a mirror to that of Clarence, his first victim in the play. Even if Richard has found literal mirrors to be unexpectedly benign, the mirror structure, in its implications of fatality, is intrinsically threatening. Both the brothers are visited, on the eve of their death, by dreams and by the ghosts of their past crimes.[4] Clarence's speech is in two parts, two distinct dreams. The first moves from a guilty, and entirely clear-sighted, memory of events, to an expression of his vivid fear of Richard, whom in 'waking' situations Clarence, as we have seen from the first encounter in the play, still trusts. The second is a ghostly visitation. That first part is readable in common-sense terms as a processing of the anxiety that shapes Clarence's situation.

> KEEPER  What was your dream, my lord? I pray you tell me.
> CLARENCE  Methoughts that I had broken from the Tower
> And was embark'd to cross to Burgundy;
> And in my company my brother Gloucester,
> Who from my cabin tempted me to walk
> Upon the hatches: thence we look'd toward England,
> And cited up a thousand heavy times,
> During the wars of York and Lancaster,
> That had befall'n us. As we pac'd along
> Upon the giddy footing of the hatches,
> Methought that Gloucester stumbled, and in falling,
> Struck me (that thought to stay him) overboard,
> Into the tumbling billows of the main.
>
> (I.iv.8–20)

Stephen Greenblatt has recently drawn attention to the intersection between dream experience and historical anxiety particularly in situations of tyranny. What cannot be directly admitted resurfaces in the symbolism of dreams.[5] Here sleep gives Clarence some respite from the effort of a strenuous self-censorship. His guilt at his earlier betrayal of his family manifests itself in an inability to admit the possibility that his brother too might be treacherous. The second part of the dream – recounted after his interlocutor points out that Clarence should, logically have woken from a dream of drowning and choking – is more in the nature of a vision, a divinely sent judgement, coming in from outside the individual consciousness, and opening up a wider, a metaphysical, arena.

> Then came wand'ring by
> A shadow like an angel, with bright hair
> Dabbled in blood; and he shriek'd out aloud,
> 'Clarence is come: false, fleeting, perjur'd Clarence,
> That stabb'd me in the field by Tewkesbury!
> Seize on him, Furies! Take him unto torment!'

(I.iv.52–7)

In the Quartos (typical of their economical story telling), the 'keeper' is Brackenbury, the lieutenant of the Tower, who stays on stage until the murderers arrive; this is the option almost all productions take, but the Folio has a separate, more menial 'keeper' to talk to Clarence. In that text, Brackenbury arrives to point a moral over the sleeping man:

> Princes have but their titles for their glories,
> An outward honour for an inward toil;
> And, for unfelt imagination,
> They often feel a world of restless cares:
> So that, betwixt their titles and low name,
> There's nothing differs but the outward fame.

(I.vi.74–9)

Though the sentiment and the closing couplet are trite, Brackenbury's meditation on 'unfelt imagination' takes us close to a central concern of the play. The phrase is a difficult one. 'Imagination' may not involve feeling in the tactile, experiential sense, but it allows us to 'feel' a 'world', a totalizing experience like the image in a convex mirror, of our world rendered emotionally intelligible, and so only too accessible to feeling in the larger non-material sense. When the murderers arrive, Brackenbury demonstrates to us the nature of the play's waking world:

> I will not reason what is meant hereby,
> Because I will be guiltless from the meaning.
> There lies the Duke asleep; and there the keys.

88

> I'll to the King; and signify to him
> That thus I have resign'd to you my charge.

(I.iv.94–8)

Brackenbury's poise derives from a complex intuition – to reason is dangerous in this world, as it involves inviting the crimes that condition it into consciousness. It is safer to mark decisively where ones own moral responsibility ends. But this is at the cost of a willed self-repression. What does Brackenbury dream of?

## BE NOT AFRAID OF SHADOWS

Mirrors can be bought, smashed at will, looked at or not looked at, but the shadow cannot be so easily dismissed. If one can acknowledge, celebrate, even 'court' one's reflection, a shadow always takes one by surprise; it is unsought, unpredictable, it changes in scale and in the angle of our relation to it. It is not in our control.[6] That Richard is thrown back on having to acknowledge it in his situation at the start of the play is a mark of his desperation.

> ... I, in this weak piping time of peace,
> Have no delight to pass away the time,
> Unless to spy my shadow in the sun,
> And descant on mine own deformity.

(I.i.24–7)

He 'spies' his shadow – he looks at it askance, surreptitiously. A sense of the shadow, both as threatening to us, and, as a reminder of self to Richard, as the will moving forward towards its ends, is developed throughout the Olivier film, and has been invoked to some extent in almost every staging since. In a twentieth-century context, the 'shadow' idea has a cinematic heritage going back to the European expressionistic movies of the early part of the century; in Carl Dreyer's *Vampyr*, for example, the vampire's shadow moves independently of him; in the climactic scene of *Nosferatu* we see not him but his shadow moving up the stairs, anticipating his desires for his victims.[7] This has its philosophical rationale in Jung's idea of the shadow, the accumulated negative capacity of a being, a source of malign power.[8] A shadow is, of course, that which is not light; Richard's 'shine out fair sun' (I.i.262) is itself a triumphant conquering of the resented 'sun' (the regal and libidinous Edward, his envied anti-type), which, given his flattering mirror in Anne, he can order about, and need not fear.

Shadows, in Elizabethan terms, – the terms of Puck's 'If we shadows have offended' in his epilogue to *A Midsummer's Night's Dream* – are also ghosts, spirits, actors. This sense and the literal sense find a congruence in Richard's dream on the eve of Bosworth.[9] The ghostly shadows there are shadows cast by Richard, the unwilled return of his past deeds; they are of him, and not of him, the silhouette of a moral deformity. On the eve of Bosworth we see the ghosts, the 'shadows' of all those Richard killed – including Edward, Henry's son (the 'angel' of Clarence's dream), and Henry himself, killed before this play has begun. They visit Richard as he sleeps, and Richmond. Like the ghosts of the second part of Clarence's dream, they belong more to the world of 'vision', of a moral and prophetic visitation from another world, than to the dream-work of individual psychology.

This sheer accumulation of figures presents a challenge to the director, which some (Mendes, Pimlott) have dealt with by stylizing the conference of ghosts as a kind of last supper, or macabre banquet. Productions, understandably, tend to limit the ghosts to those seen alive in this play, but there is an added resonance when, in a 'cycle' presentation' like the Lesser/Noble instatement of the play as the climax of *The Plantagenets*, the ghost Henry can not only appear, but be played by as important an actor as Ralph Fiennes; there is a sense then of the whole saga drawing to a close. The frontispiece to Nicholas Rowe's 1709 edition has a comically pissed-off looking Richard seated, asleep, with his elbow on a table and his head resting on his hand. The ghosts are in shrouds tied, as was the practice, in a knot on their heads, like badly wrapped Christmas crackers. If, as has often been suggested, these illustrations are based on stage practice, then this suggests a grotesquely humorous interpretation.[10] It points to the difficult balancing act that directors and designers must perform in order to realize the scene visually. The scene has both to suggest the threat of a vengeful mob, and to remain not quite corporeal. There must be some sense of awe, but at the same time there is a kind of sick humour, a release of comic energy, in so flamboyantly literal a rebellion of Richard's victims.The Rodway/Hands production drew on the visual conventions of Holbein's *Dance of Death* to suggest this, as an armoured deathshead led the ghosts out by the hand after the battle. In the BBC/S4C *Richard III*, in the series 'Shakespeare: The Animated Tales', a Russian/Welsh co-production, scripted by Leon Garfield and directed by Natalia Orlova, the visual style of the cartoon animation inhabits the expressionist/gothic area that circumscribes much of the late-nineteenth- and twentieth-century reception of the play, and its graphic conventions allow an elegant and concise realization of the scene. As the printed text has it: 'Richard is alone in his tent. He sits wearily down on his bed and drinks a glass of wine in one gulp. He puts the glass on the table and watches the light of the lamp. He sleeps. The lamp begins to burn blue. Strange, flimsy white wisps enter the tent. They gather round the sleeping king. Little by little, they assume more definite shapes. They are the ghosts of his victims. They go in circles above Richard, one by one coming closer to him. Richard stirs and tosses in his sleep.'[11] This is sensitively derived from the text – the distraught Elizabeth's 'If yet your gentle souls fly in the air/ ... Hover about me with your airy wings', and the Duchess of York's 'the little souls of Edward's children/Whisper the spirits of thine enemies' is realized at Richard's death: 'He raises his sword. The air is full of whispers. He strikes out, but his sword is heavy. Richmond in a single blow cuts off Richard's head'.[12] The McKellen/Loncraine film loses the scene to give Richard a more generalized kind of troubled night and allows Richmond's correspondingly cheerful waking to be the expression of his satisfaction in his wedding night with the nubile teenaged Elizabeth of York. More tellingly, perhaps picking up on Emrys Jones's remark in *Looking for Richard* that 'for Richard, the ghosts are the battle', the Lindsay/Moshinsky version moved the appearance of the ghosts to the fight between Richard and Richmond, in an exciting choreographed sequence, where the more mobile of the victims interposed themselves between Richard's sword and an out-fought Richmond to tell their murderer to 'despair and die'.

However the scene is staged, the ghosts appear as the return of what Richard has chosen to repress. In taking an externalized and fully visible form, they are also a kind of challenge to what we think history is – they represent history the way the scenes of Clarence's children, or that of the lamenting queens do, as a kind of roll-call of victims. Richard's personal version of history is simply the narrative of his progress towards the throne. The ghosts are not simply part of Richard's psychology – the film versions make them seem like this, but that is the nature of film as a medium, where we have got used to an intercutting of (as in the Pacino film) Richard tossing on his bed, with visually distorted images of the other characters. On the stage, where we see Richmond, and Richard and the ghosts in the same space, the effect is of a new perspective on the action. The stage space, unusually in Shakespeare, moves out of the 'realistic' mode of the rest of the play, in presenting both camps on stage at the same time.[13] The Elizabethan stage was in natural light, and the audience visible both to the actors and to each other. From the claustrophobic pulling in of focus on Richard's tent, which stands in for the interior of his mind, for his secret thoughts, we become aware of a space like the space of the moral world, in which events cannot be hidden from the judging eye. The rhetoric of the play instates this as the eye of God, but, excitingly, it gives it to us as our position of spectatorship. It is Richmond himself who invokes the perspective of God:

> O Thou, whose captain I account myself,
> Look on my forces with a gracious eye;
> Put in their hands Thy bruising irons of wrath
> That they may crush down, with a heavy fall,
> Th'usurping helmets of our adversaries;
> Make us Thy ministers of chastisement,
> That we may praise Thee in the victory.
> To Thee I do commend my watchful soul
> Ere I let fall the windows of mine eyes:
> Sleeping and waking, O defend me still!

> (V.iii.109–18)

Then the ghosts enter. From now on points of view can no longer be partial. Distortions seem to disappear, the anamorphic shape may soon be readable from the 'right' angle. We are now no longer the 'apprentice Richards'[14] of our reception of the early soliloquies, but are placed above an increasingly confused and futile action, and offerered the chance to set things on the right course – if we assent to Richard's adversary.

## RICHARD STARTS OUT OF HIS DREAM

The English painter William Hogarth achieved the grandeur that eluded most of Boydell's painters in his portrait of David Garrick as Richard III, now in the Walker Art Gallery, Liverpool. The studied composition and rich palette of the picture invest a theatrical portrait with the power and complexity of the Italian 'old masters' so admired at the time, and the source, to the English, of a cultural inferiority complex. The very existence of the picture is a token of the way Garrick had changed the perceived status of the actor. Hogarth implicitly acknowledges him as an equal, a partner in the aesthetic project of creating a moralized realism, the robust rendering of daily life and social behaviour as the medium of a more accessible and democratic art. Richard was Garrick's breakthrough role. It is perhaps ironic that, while the performance was hailed as a rediscovery of the true qualities of Shakespeare, Garrick performed in Cibber's text. It was 'character' that interested Garrick and his audiences, and Cibber, in producing a more securely central, a more psychologically coherent, even more admirable figure, was, as far as theatrical tradition was concerned, more Shakespearean than Shakespeare. Garrick excelled at moments of vision, confrontations with the 'other'.[15] Here the 'other' is himself.

> *Richard starteth out of his dream*
> K RICHARD Give me another horse! Bind up my wounds!
> Have mercy, Jesu! – Soft! I did but dream.
> O coward conscience, how dost thou afflict me!
> The lights burn blue. It is now dead midnight.
> Cold fearful drops stand on my trembling flesh.

(V.iii.178–82)

Cibber cut the speech down to nine lines; those quoted above remain much the same, but the order is different, and 'coward conscience' becomes 'Tyrant Conscience', and the end of the speech has a more 'heroic' ring which might remind one of Byron's empathetic reaction to the role ('Richard was a man');[16]

this distinctly 'Byronic' sentiment, not Shakespeare's continuation of the speech, is what Byron would have heard:

> When I look back, 'tis terrible Retreating:
> I cannot bear the thought, nor dare repent:
> I am but Man, and Fate, do thou dispose me.[17]

Garrick, in that ambiguous state between sleep and waking, clutched his sword automatically, and struggled out of the dream into the waking world.[18] Hogarth uses the conventions of 'history painting' – a language of visual symbolism partly derived from Renaissance religious painting – to realize Shakespeare's vision more fully. That 'The lights burn blue' indicates the presence of a ghost.[19] Hogarth renders this, suggesting he had gone back to read Shakespeare (Cibber had cut it), but his main focus is on the startled look in Richard/Garrick's eyes, and his outstretched hand, a favourite convention in Hogarth's work to convey terror; it both fends off and acknowledges something seen by the protagonist, but not the viewer.[20] Armour lies strewn at Richard's feet, blue flowers, perhaps sage, or bugle, representing melancholy, accompany red flowers reminiscent of the briar roses that (in *King Henry the Sixth, Part I*) started the whole thing off. Richmond's tents are seen in a warm – or from Richard's point of view, ominously fiery – dawn glow. This again suggests that Hogarth had looked at Shakespeare, who contradicts the 'dead midnight' with Stanley's somewhat earlier 'flaky darkness breaks within the East' (V.iii.181, 87). It is of course symbolic that Richmond's supporters see a dawn that Richard cannot, and it is typical of Shakespeare that the scene works from two senses of time simultaneously. Richard's is frozen in a nightmare, Richmond's moves briskly and clearly on towards dawn.

One of Hogarth's most striking details – picking up on 'Have mercy, Jesu!' (V.iii.179) – is the crucifix behind Richard's left shoulder. It is striking partly because it is visually highly ambiguous. It is in a frame, which renders it unclear whether it is two- or three-dimensional; it may even be incorporeal. The frame might be a mirror, in which the cross has appeared; a reflection that comments on Richard's lack of 'reflection' in another sense, for, whatever it is, he has his back to it, spurning repentance.

Illustration 7   William Hogarth, *Garrick as Richard III*

Richard's language creates a mirror to himself, but the repetition can sound sterile, almost comic:

> What do I fear? Myself? There's none else by;
> Richard loves Richard, that is, I am I.[21]
> Is there a murderer here? No. Yes, I am!
> Then fly. What, from myself? Great reason why,
> Lest I revenge? What, myself upon myself?
> Alack, I love myself. Wherefore? For any good
> That I myself have done unto myself?
> O no, alas, I rather hate myself
> For hateful deeds committed by myself.
> I am a villain – Yet I lie, I am not!
> Fool, of thyself speak well! Fool, do not flatter.

> (V.iii.183–93)

Robert Lindsay was attacked by a fit of rather hollow sounding giggles at 'Yes, I am', an effect in tune with a characterization of a misfit Richard in whom nervous fear and hilarity were never far away from each other. In his preparation for the battle, Lindsay pitched 'I would these dewy tears were from the ground' (V.iii.285) as a wail of fear, while brushing tears way from his own eyes. This is simply a misreading of 'from', which in Elizabethan terms means 'away from'. Richard is saying that he would rather not fight on damp ground. But it reminds us of Richard's previous block on tears, in his reaction to the death of his father and of his young brother Rutland (*Henry the Sixth, Part III*, II.i.81–6) as well as his celebration of the impassive murderers. Perhaps these tears are 'from' Richard in the modern sense as well.

## 'I SEE AS IN A MAP, THE END OF ALL'

Queen Elizabeth's reaction to news of her brothers' arrest was to exclaim,

> Ay me! I see the ruin of my House:
> The tiger now hath seiz'd the gentle hind;
> Insulting tyranny begins to jut
> Upon the innocent and aweless throne.
> Welcome destruction, blood, and massacre;
> I see, as in a map, the end of all.

> (II.iv.49–54)

Elizabeth's clear-sighted – if inevitably, at this point, pessimistic – perspective on the political possibilities open to her comes to coincide at the end of the play with Richmond's construction of the eye of God looking over all. As Elizabeth steers her daughter away from Richard and to Richmond, there is the sense of an opening up, a return to true perspective, an end of the nightmare. Perhaps 'the end of all' is not to be to her disadvantage after all. I said earlier that Elizabeth 'seemed' to escape from Richard. Cibber's version gives her an aside to clarify this: 'By sending Richmond Word of his Intent,/Shall gain some time to let my child escape him./It shall be so'.[22] But in Hall (More's account ends before it reaches this point) Elizabeth is finally persuaded by Richard.[23] Productions, like critics,[24] have been more or less equally split between readings where Elizabeth is defeated, as Brenda Bruce was in the Rodway/Hands performances, or escapes with her daughter, like Annette Benning in the McKellen/Loncraine one. In the Lesser/Noble production, the pathetic, brutalized doll-clutching figure of Elizabeth means that the issue is left open, as an index of the character's own confusion.

The dramatic point of the scene must surely depend on a degree of contrast to the wooing of Anne, and the 'mirror' structure that underlines Richard's diminishing power would suggest, as would the greater evasiveness of Elizabeth's language, that Richard has here been outsmarted. But what happens to Elizabeth at the end of the play is ambiguous, and this ambiguity reflects a historical moment both decisive and mysterious. Both Tey and Weir have problems with the psychology of the historical Elizabeth Woodville.[25] For Tey the historical evidence of Elizabeth's support for a match with Richard is clinching evidence that Richard could not have killed the princes – else how could Elizabeth agree, as she did at one stage, to the betrothal to him of her daughter? But one cannot solve a historical enigma by importing back into it the normative psychology of one's own period. The historical Elizabeth Woodville was a powerful and ambitious figure, whom the Elizabethans seem to have been as hard put to interpret as we are ourselves. She seems to have tried to marry her daughter off to either Richard or Richmond; which of the two it was at the time was contingent on her own situation. The courts of Europe were rife with gossip – which Henry VII/Richmond's later behaviour would seem to substantiate in his hostility to both wife and mother in law – that Elizabeth of York was, with her mother's consent, conducting an incestuous affair with Richard. At one Christmas banquet, shortly before Anne died, Elizabeth turned up at court in the same highly expensive dress as the queen, and sat to dine at her 'uncle's' side.[26]

Elizabeth of York is one of the three women powerful in the narrative of the play but silent and invisible in the early staging texts. As in the case of Jane Shore, modern productions tend to create a role for her. The third is Stanley's wife, and Richmond's mother, Margaret, alluded to threateningly by Richard (IV.ii.86), and in historical terms the real power behind the final resolution of the conflict.[27] Many productions have Elizabeth of York entering with the Duchess of York at the start of IV.i to meet Elizabeth at the Tower, replacing Margaret, Clarence's daughter, whom all the early texts indicate here. Unless we take Margaret to be visiting the site of her father's death, there is little point to her being here.[28] Elizabeth of York often appears again in the last scene of the play. Pacino has Queen Elizabeth, a silent figure who presumably represents Elizabeth of York, and the Duchess of York and Margaret watching the final battle from the top of a hill, a neat return to Elizabeth's 'I see as in a map'.

## 'WHAT TRAITOR HEARS ME...?'

The play may finally seem to instate a sense of the rightness of Richmond's victory, and the providential pattern which underlies it as 'historical truth'.

> Proclaim a pardon to the soldiers fled
> That in submission will return to us;
> And then, as we have ta'en the sacrament,
> We will unite the white rose and the red.
> Smile, heaven, upon this fair conjunction,
> That long have frown'd upon their enmity!
> What traitor hears me and says not Amen?
>
> (V.v.16–19)

But this is done through a reference to a heraldic symbolism – of the roses – of a kind which the violence and sheer contingency of the preceding action has devalued. And that last line is more than a little threatening – of course no one is going to want to define themselves as a traitor by denying the new military victor the assent he wants. We are reminded that power and military force determine what is or is not a successful rhetoric.

The Jarvis/Bogdanov production made exciting and intelligent theatre out of this issue. The cycle of which the performance was a part had moved in eclectic costume and design through from the early nineteenth century to the present day. The climactic battle between Richmond and Richard was thrillingly staged as a dream of the middle ages (McKellen/Eyre also moved into armour for this moment, but without any clear thesis), with Richmond in golden armour, accompanied by nostalgic Elgarian music. But Richmond's final speech was given from a TV studio, where Elizabeth and her daughter sat beside him, a setting which exposed the manufacturedness of the dream of England's 'last battle' – these are all 'images', thrown at us with a design on soliciting our support and belief; they are part of the way the play explores the role in history of the manufacture of images and texts, the power those images and texts have, despite perhaps the scepticism we may have about them simultaneous with our consumption of them.

I realize that in talking about this play I have been persistently led away from trying to establish anything we can see as a fixed unquestionable truth – truth in historical terms, in terms of any one production's fidelity to the text, in terms of the stability of the texts themselves. I think this is the nature of the play, and the source of its excitement. It leads us down a labyrinth of research, from which, like Josephine Tey's hospital-bound detective, we may emerge with a healthy scepticism as to how history is 'made' for us – a reminder that it is a construct, not a given. If the English adage Tey cites asserts that 'truth is the daughter of time' and so will, in time, be engendered, a contemporary Flemish proverb makes an opposite point, though one equally accessible to common sense; that the daughter of time is forgetfulness.[29] The space between these two warring daughters is a space in which desire – the audience's desire - spins stories of its own.

The Olivier film begins in this vein; with a kind of disclaimer – what it presents is a 'legend'. It cuts Richmond's speech, ending instead with an image that brilliantly takes us both to the destabilizing uncertainty of the ending of the Jarvis/ Bogdanov production, and to the kind of speculation raised by Freud, and by Bill Alexander – the director of the production in which Antony Sher starred – who characterized the audience as 'trainee Richards'. The film returns throughout to an image of an outsize crown suspended over the coronation seat, often echoed visually in the gestures of characters, either crowned or replacing their ducal coronets on their heads. When Stanley, in the final wordless moments of the film, offers the crown to Richmond, he is unseen; it is offered to us as the audience, for the cameras point of view is at this point both ours and his. We look up, the crown comes down, as if on to *our* head. Then its image is replaced by that of the outsize crown that forms a baldachin over the coronation throne – a repeated motif in the film. Then the photographic image is in its turn replaced by a graphic image, placed – ominously? or hesitantly? – between the words 'The' and 'End'.

# Notes

## INTRODUCTION

1. The British television channel C4 ran *The Trial of Richard III*, a court case following current British law and using all the available evidence for the historical Richard's guilt. He was found not guilty by a jury. The proceedings were published as Richard Drewett and Mark Redhead's *The Trial of Richard III* (Gloucester: Alan Sutton, 1984).

2. George Buck, *The History of King Richard the Third* (1619), ed. Arthur Noel Kincaid (Gloucester: Alan Sutton, 1982).

3. The controversy was sparked off in this case by the news that Bell had received some money from the publishers of Gitta Sereny's book about her, *Cries Unheard: The Story of Mary Bell* (London; Macmillan 1998).

4. Antony Sher, *Year of the King* (London: Methuen, 1985), 97.

5. *King Richard the Third*, ed. E. A. J. Honigmann (Harmondsworth: Penguin, 1968), 25–30.

6. Hammond, in the Arden edition (Introduction, pp. 1–50), gives a very full and fair account of the theories of genesis of the various texts. In summary, D. L. Patrick, in *The Textual History of Richard III* (Stanford, 1936), gave an argument for memorial reconstruction, which was accepted until Kristian Smidt (Oslo, 1964) suggested that the text was derived from a prompt book, which in itself represents a revision for performance of a text more fully reproduced in the Folio. This seems to me more likely. In the Quarto's version, more obviously derived from memory, it is often clear who the 'culprits' were. In the bad Quarto of *Hamlet*, for example, it was obviously Horatio and Laertes, who get their own lines right and garble everyone else's.

7. Colley Cibber, *The Tragical History of King Richard the Third* (London, 1718; London: Cornmarket Press facsimile, 1969), 25–6.

8. Hugh Richmond, for example, asserts that 'many members of the

first audience which saw *Richard III* may have acquired this feeling of a larger context, because they had been exposed to the whole of *Henry VI*...thus the RSC restored a sense of continuity in the audience's responses to the original performance of *Richard III*... Perhaps for the first time in centuries, *Richard III* was fully restored to its generic character as an Elizabethan history play'. *Shakespeare in Performance: King Richard III* (Manchester: Manchester University Press, 1989), 72–4.

9. As Tillyard puts it, in E. M. W. Tillyard, *Shakespeare's History Plays* (London: Chatto and Windus, 1944), 'Behind disorder is some sort of order or "degree" on earth, and that order has its counterpart in heaven. This assertion has nothing to do with the question of Shakespeare's personal piety: it merely means that Shakespeare used the thought-idiom of his age' (p. 8). *Richard III* and the *Henry VI* plays are for him united by 'the steady political theme: the theme of order and chaos, of proper political degree and civil war, of crime and punishment, of God's mercy finally tempering his justice, of the belief that such had been God's way with England' (pp. 200–201). According to Lily B. Campbell, in *Shakespeare's Histories: Mirrors of Elizabethan Policy* (San Marino, CA: The Huntingdon Library, 1947), 'An usurper seizes the throne; God avenges his sin upon the third heir through the agency of another usurper, whose sin is again avenged upon the third heir...the understanding of the moral significance of this pattern is basic to the understanding of the Shakespeare history sequences' (pp. 122–4).

10. A. P. Rossiter argues, in *Angel with Horns, and other Shakespeare Lectures*, ed. Graham Storey (London: Longmans, 1961), that, 'had he entirely accepted the Tudor myth, the frame and pattern of order, his way would have led, I suppose, towards writing *moral history* (which is what Dr Tillyard and Dr Dover Wilson and Professor Duthie have made out of him). Instead, his way led him towards writing *comic history*. The former would never have taken him to tragedy: the latter (paradoxically) did' (p. 22). According to John Wilders in *The Lost Garden: A View of Shakespeare's English and Roman History Plays* (London: Macmillan, 1978), 'The causes of national unity or division, of prosperity or decline are, in Shakespeare's view, to be found not, as some of the fifteenth century chroniclers had believed, in the providential powers of God, nor, as we are now inclined to think, in social and economic conditions, but in the temperaments of national leaders and their reactions to one another' (p. 2).

11. According to the actor Richard Pearson, Peter Hall referred to Kott's formulation of 'the Grand Mechanism' in the context of the controversy "history has a meaning" v. "history has no meaning"' – Richard Pearson, *'A Band of Arrogant and United Heroes': The Story of*

*the Royal Shakespeare Company Production of 'The Wars of the Roses'* (London: Adelphi Press, 1990), 26–7, 52; Jan Kott, *Shakespeare Our Contemporary*, trans. Boleslaw Taborski (London: Methuen, 1964), 7.

12. Emrys Jones makes the most sophisticated connection between Shakespeare and the Mysteries in *The Origins of Shakespeare* (Oxford: Oxford University Press, 1977), 31–84. He carefully styles their influence as a matter of 'forms and patterns of thought and feeling, a largely unconscious and unfocused inheritance from pre-Reformation England' (p. 33).

13. Freud derives an interpretation of Richard from two case studies of patients who had 'found' a congenital reason for things they felt were holding them back in life: 'we feel that we ourselves might become like Richard, that on a small scale, indeed, we are already like him. Richard is an enormous magnification of something we find in ourselves as well...we all think we have reason to reproach Nature and our destiny for congenital and infantile disadvantages' – M. D. Faber, *The Design Within* (New York: Science House, 1970), 34–5. Robert Ravich, in 'A Psychoanalytic Study of Shakespeare's Early Plays', *Psychoanalytic Quarterly*, 33 (1964), extends Freud's ideas and applies them to other Shakespearean plays.

14. Sher, *Year of the King*, 172, 185, 206.

15. Julie Hankey, *Richard III: Plays in Performance* (London: Junction Books, 1981), 76–7.

16. Susan Fossiter, Ashok Roy and Marin Wyld, *Making and Meaning: Holbein's Ambassadors* (London: National Gallery Publications, 1997), 30–43.

17. Stephen Greenblatt, *Renaissance Self-Fashioning: From More to Shakespeare* (Chicago and London: The University of Chicago Press, 1980), 25; *Making and Meaning*, 43.

18. Honigmann, 12.

19. *Making and Meaning*, 50.

## CHAPTER 1.   THE BODY

1. The idea is ultimately derived from the Latin aesthetic theorist Vitruvius, from his *The Ten Books on Architecture*, Bk III, I, ii ('On symmetry: in temples and in the human body').

2. Mikhail Bakhtin, *Rabelais and his World*, trans. Helene Iswolsky (Bloomington: Indiana University Press, 1984), 28–9.

3. The image was projected onto a transparent front curtain at the beginning of *Pericles*, and imitated in a spectacular coup-de-théâtre as a suddenly apparent three-dimensional image of 'Time', revolving in a mirrored cube at the beginning of *The Winter's Tale*.

4. Thomas S. Freeman traces the influence of classical historiography through Shakespeare's sources into the play, in 'From Catiline to *Richard III*: The Influence of Classical Historians on Polydore Vergil's *Anglica Historia*', in Mario A. Di Cesare (ed.) *Reconsidering the Renaissance* (New York: Mediaeval and Renaissance Texts and Studies (1992), vol. 93). His emphasis on anecdote and invented speech is especially relevant here (pp. 194–7).

5. The text here, and throughout, is my own modernization of More's English version (henceforth More), as given in *The Complete Works of St Thomas More*, vol. 2, ed. Richard S. Sylvester (New Haven: Yale University Press, 1963), 6–7.

6. For Harry Levin, in 'Two Tents on Bosworth Field: *Richard III* V.iii.v', it is the soliloquies of *Henry the Sixth, Part III* that strike us as distinctly Marlovian ... *Richard III* has become more typically Shakespearean in its succinct formulation, its structural equilibrium and its psychological modality', Jonathan Hart (ed.) *Reading the Renaissance: Culture, Poetics and Drama* (New York: Garland, 1996), 151.

7. Sher, *Year of the King*, 189–91.

8. Ibid., 108–17.

9. Ibid., 172.

10. Ibid.: 'It seems terribly unfair of Shakespeare to begin his play with such a famous speech' (p. 27).

11. The Riverside edition, normally used in this essay for plays other than *Richard III*, omits this line, on the basis that it is found only in the Quartos.

12. See Hankey, *Richard III: Plays in Performance*, 90

13. Constantin Stanislavski set out his theories and rehearsal practices (derived largely from his sense of his own shortcomings as an actor) most influentially in his semi-fictional narrative *An Actor Prepares*, first translated into English in 1937.

14. Sher, *Year of the King*, 22, and throughout.

15. Quoted from Honigmann, *King Richard the Third*, 7.

16. Charles Dickens, *The Old Curiosity Shop* (first published as a weekly serial, April 1840–February 1841; first published in book form in February 1841.) See, in this context chapters 4–6.

17. Pauline Kael, *At the Movies* (New York: Dutton, 1994), 1216; originally a review for the *New Yorker*, October, 1987.

18. Ryder's casting is inspired, in line with her roles in Tim Burton's *Beetlejuice* and *Edward Scissorhands* and in Coppola's *Bram Stoker's Dracula*, as the intelligent, discontented but inexperienced girl gradually drawn into becoming the lover/confidante of 'the monster'.

19. According to Marguerite Waller, Richard is 'a relatively common species of manipulative narcissist'. See 'Usurpation, Seduction, and

the Problematics of the Proper: A "Deconstuctive" "Feminist" Rereading of the Seductions of Anne and Richard in Shakespeare's *Richard III'*, in Margaret W. Ferguson, Maureen Quilligan and Nancy J. Vickers (eds.) *Rewriting the Renaissance: The Discourses of Sexual Difference in Early Modern Europe* (Chicago: University of Chicago Press, 1986), 145–58. She goes on to say that 'Richard's role in the seduction of Anne is, thus, less self-initiated than it might at first appear. In a sense it is written for him, in Anne's discourse, before he ever approaches her. He need only respond to the double nature of her bereavement – her loss of her male points of reference and her role as a subjectivity that thinks of *itself* as authoritative' (p. 172).

20. For Coleridge, according to a report of his lectures of 1808, 'he declared his conviction that no part of Richard the 3d except the character of Richard was written by S., doubtless with a silent reference to the disgusting character of Lady Anne'. See *Coleridge's Shakespeare Criticism*, ed. Thomas Middleton Raysor (London: Constable, 1930) vol. II, p. 16. Disgusting has less force than it has today, with a meaning rather more like 'distasteful'. In a rare slip, the Garland bibliography, *Richard III: An Annotated Bibliography*, compiled by James A. Moore (New York and London, Garland, 1986), ascribes the same opinion to Samuel Johnson (p, 245), but Johnson is actually talking about the 'wooing' of Elizabeth, which he takes to be a success for Richard. See below, ch. 5, 'Mirrors and Shadows', n. 24.

21. Kott, *Shakespeare Our Contemporary*: 'one of the greatest scenes written by Shakespeare, and one of the greatest ever written ... Lady Anne knows well what times she is living in' (pp. 35–6).

22. Marilyn French, *Shakespeare's Division of Experience* (New York Summit Books, 1981), 43–75. See also, in addition to Waller (n.19, above), Coppelia Kahn, in *Man's Estate: Masculine Identity in Shakespeare* (Berkeley: University of California Press, 1981) which focuses on the role of the family, and of 'alienation from the mother' in the formation of Richard's character (pp. 63–6), and Madonne. M. Miner ' "Neither mother, wife, nor England's queen": The Roles of Women in *Richard III'*, in Carolyn Ruth Swift Lennz, Gayle Greene, and Carol Thomas Neely (eds.) *The Woman's Part: Feminist Criticism of Shakespeare*, (Urbana: University of Illinois Press, 35–55).

23. See Scott Colley, *Richard's Himself Again: A Stage History of Richard III* (New York: Greenwood Press, 1992), for an account of the various Moriarty productions (pp. 211–15).

24. Moore, *Richard III; An Annotated Bibliography*, p. xxxix.

25. Richard Burt, 'The Love that dare not speak Shakespeare's name: New Shakesqueer cinema', in Linda E. Boose (ed.) *Shakespeare, the Movie: Popularizing the Plays in Film, TV and Radio* (London: Routledge, 1997), 240–66, ref. at p. 257.

26. Alison Weir, *The Princes in the Tower* (London: Pimlico, 1992).
27. Sher, *Year of the King*, 90–1.
28. Dickens, *The Old Curiosity Shop* (see n.16 above). Michael Steig extends the comparison to Oskar Matzerath, in Günter Grass's *The Tin Drum* (and thence to Nazi Germany), in 'The Grotesque and the Aesthetic Response in Shakespeare, Dickens, and Günter Grass', in *Comparative Literary Studies*, 6 (1970), 167–81.

## CHAPTER 2.   DEFORMATIONS OF HISTORY

1. Pamela Tudor-Craig, *Richard III* (London: National Portrait Gallery 1973), 93.
2. Ibid., 88.
3. Horace Walpole, *Historic Doubts on the Life and Reign of King Richard the Third* (1768), ed. P. W. Hammond (Gloucester: Alan Sutton, 1987), 15.
4. Ibid., 9.
5. Ibid., 12–13.
6. Josephine Tey, *The Daughter of Time* (Harmondsworth: Penguin, 1951). Two earlier twentieth-century English novels, *Dickon*, by Marjorie Bowen, and *Crouchback*, by Carola Oman, had been published by the same publisher (Hodder and Stoughton) in the same year (1929): the first, by a prolific historical novelist, telling Richard's story from a point of view sympathetic to him; the second, by a novelist and biographer, taking the opposite tack.
7. Weir, *The Princes in the Tower*, 10. Walpole makes a similar point, but overrides it by saying that More wrote 'to amuse his leisure and exercise his fancy' (*Historic Doubts*, 26).
8. Michael Hattaway makes this point in relation to the *Henry VI* plays, in the introduction to his edition of *The First Part of King Henry the Sixth* (Cambridge: Cambridge University Press, 1990), 56–7.
9. Mandy Rice-Davies was one of two fashionable part-time prostitutes (with Christine Keeler) who were involved both with the British defence secretary of the Conservative government of the early 1960s and with a Soviet naval attaché. He denied the affair in Parliament; Ms Rice-Davies made her remark in the ensuing trial. It has passed into proverbial English usage, and into the *Oxford Dictionary of Quotations*.
10. John Arden, *To Present the Pretence: Essays on the Theatre and its Public* (London: Eyre Methuen, 1977), 195–8. Arden is citing Peter Brook on *A Midsummer Night's Dream*, while applying to the political what he takes, in Brook, to refer to the subconscious.
11. In 1979–80, the controversy as to the 'providential' reading of the play re-erupted with Robert P. Merrix, in *Studies in English Literature*,

19 (1979), 179–96, and Paul N. Siegel, in 'Tillyard Lives: Historicism and Shakespeare's History Plays', *Clio*, 9 (1979), 5–23, both of whom argue that reaction against Tillyard's views have gone too far, and Henry Ansgar Kelly, in 'Tillyard and History: Comment and Response', *Clio*, vol. 10, no. 1 (1980), answering that Tillyard is faulty, in that Margaret's curses cannot be taken to represent the will of God, and that nobody claims in the play that the death of the princes is retributive.

12. Brian Cox, *The Lear Diaries: The Story of the Royal National Theatre Productions of Shakespeare's 'Richard III' and 'King Lear'* (London: Methuen, 1992), 34.

13. Deborah Willis, in 'Shakespeare and the English Witch-Hunts: Enclosing the Maternal Body' (in *Enclosure Acts: Sexuality, Property and Culture in Early Modern England*, ed. Richard Burt and John Michael Archer (Ithaca: Cornell University Press, 1994), 96–120), argues in relation to Margaret and the Duchess of York, that 'the first tetralogy...inscribes the mother in the witch and the witch in the mother...If at first the plays seem to substitute mother-hunting for witch-hunting – inviting the audience to take pleasure in Richard's revenge on women while at the same time recognizing his misogyny – by the end of the tetralogy the witchy behaviour of the women has taken on a more positive value' (p. 102). David Sundelson, in *Shakespeare's Restorations of the Father*, (New Brunswick, NJ: Ruttgers University Press, 1983), sees Richard as characterizing women as 'castrating witches' (pp. 19–25).

14. Similar anxieties were shared by previous and subsequent regimes. See Keith Thomas, *Religion and the Decline of Magic* (London: Weidenfeld and Nicolson, 1971), 400–409.

15. For more on this, see *King Henry VI, Part I*, ed. Edward Burns (London: The Arden Shakespeare, 2000), 36–48.

16. Alice Lotvin Birney, in *Satiric Catharsis in Shakespeare: A Theory of Dramatic Structure* (Berkeley: University of California Press, 1973), argues that Margaret's curses have no power as such, but operate as a satirical outlet for the audience's feelings about Richard. In the end, though, we can't respect her, given the historical pattern of violence, in which she has played a major part (pp. 20–46). Kristian Smidt, on the other hand, argues in *Unconformities in Shakespeare's History Plays* (Highlands, NJ: Atlantic, 1982), 53–71 that Margaret's prophecies are not merely clairvoyant, but actively potent.

17. More, 54.

18. Ralph Berry points out that 'no play of Shakespeare's is so imbued with a sense of place...all London references must connect with virtually the entire audience...The place names are tiny loci of dramatic energy' ('*Richard III*: Bonding the Audience', in J. C. Gray,

(ed.), *Mirror up to Shakespeare: Essays in Honour of G. R. Hibbardd,* (Toronto: University of Toronto Press, 1984), 125.

19. Hankey, *Richard III,* 68
20. Ibid.
21. For a more positive reaction to the film than mine, see James N. Loehlin's '"TOP OF THE WORLD, MA": *Richard III* and cinematic convention' in Linda E. Boose and Richard Burt (eds.), *Shakespeare the Movie: Popularizing the Plays in Film, TV, and Video,* (London: Routledge, 1997), 67–78.
22. In his account of his conquest of Gaul, *De Bello Gallico.*
23. See Edward Burns, *Character: Acting and Being on the Pre-modern Stage* (London: Macmillan, 1991), 65–70.
24. The French novelist François Mauriac, referring to Hitler and Stalin, in his *Second Thoughts on Literature and Life,* (trans. Adrienne Foulk, London: Darwen Finlayson, 1961), says of the history plays, 'I had found them tedious before and had never really got inside them, but the drama of war that we have come through has strangely illuminated the beauty of these plays...Shakespeare has helped me to follow with my mind's eye the leading roles played in our wars, (p. 107).

## CHAPTER 3.   PLAYS AND PLAYERS

1. More, 52.
2. See *The Complete Works of St Thomas More,* vol. 4, *Utopia,* ed. Edward Louis Surtz and Jack H. Hexter (New Haven: Yale University Press, 1979).
3. See Leonard Tennenhouse, *Power on Display: The Politics of Shakespeare's Genres* (London: Methuen, 1986).
4. For Freud, see above, Introduction, n.15 and Sher, *Year of the King,* 177.
5. Cox, *The Lear Diaries,* 87 ('I realised that the production will tend to be camp, but we have to go along with it, play the thirties idea for what it is worth', p. 49).
6. Hankey, *Richard III,* 29–31.
7. E. H. Kantorowicz discusses the medieval basis for this idea in his highly influential *The King's Two Bodies: A Study in Mediaeval Political Theology* (Princeton, NJ: Princeton University Press, 1957). Marie Axton, in *The Queen's Two Bodies: Drama and the Elizabethan Succession* (London: Royal Historical Society, 1977), develops the argument in relation to Elizabeth, particularly as regards the crisis surrounding Mary Queen of Scots, and the Stuart succession.
8. For Ralph Berry, in *The Shakespearean Metaphor: Studies in Language and*

*Form* (London: Macmillan, 1978), 'A major organising metaphor for *Richard III* is the actor, together with play/audience. Obviously, the actor metaphor covers the manoeuverings of the central character. More than that, it structures the play...the first half...describes an actor immersed in role-playing, the second half shows him confronting the realities from which his playing had excluded him' (p. 9).

9. See Phillip Mallett, 'Shakespeare's Trickster-Kings: Richard III and Henry V', in Paul V. A. Williams (ed.) *The Fool and the Trickster: Studies in Honour of Enid Welsford* (Cambridge: D. S. Brewer, 1979), 64–82. For Mallett, Henry is more of a sham, and just as much a Machiavel; in Richard, 'the trickster has taken over the world of the play, and the trick has taken over the trickster' (p. 82). Anne Righter makes the comparison to the 'vice' in connection with the theme of the 'player-king',in *Shakespeare and the Idea of the Play* (London: Chatto and Windus, 1962), 96–100, as does Kenneth Muir in 'Shakespeare and the Tragic Pattern', *Proceedings of the British Academy*, 44 (1958), 145–62).

10. See Francis Hugh Mares, 'The Origin of the Figure Called "The Vice" in Tudor Drama', in *The Huntingdon Library Quarterly*, vol. XXII (1958–9), 11–29.

11. For the text of the Chester *Antichrist*, and its preceding play, *The Prophets of Antichrist*, see R. M. Lumiansky and David Mills (ed.) *The Chester Mystery Cycle* (Oxford: EETS, 1974). A conflation and adaptation of the two plays, commissioned by Chester Cathedral from the current writer, was reinstated into the cycle as directed by George Roman in 1997.

12. Weir, *The Princes in the Tower*, 5.

13. The medieval plays tend to conflate Luke 23:27–8, and its description of the 'daughters of Jerusalem' who meet Jesus and mourn for him, with the three women named in John 19:25 as 'Jesus his mother, and his mother's sister, Mary the wife of Cleophas and Mary Magdalene'.

14. Sher, *Year of the King*, 169.

15. For Kean's Richard, see Hankey, *Richard III*, 47–58.

16. *The Old Curiosity Shop*, ch. 15 (with illustration, 'Punch in the Churchyard') ch. 19. John J. McLaughlin discusses 'Richard III as Punch' in *South Carolina Review*, vol. 10, no. 1 (1977), 79–86.

## CHAPTER 4.   WOMEN AND CHILDREN

1. George Bernard Shaw, *Shaw on Shakespeare*, ed. Edwin Wilson (London: Cassell 1961), 157.

2. Hankey, *Richard III*, 65.

3. Ecclesiastes 10:15–16.
4. Sher, *Year of the King*, 183.
5. See above, n. 15 to Introduction.
6. Sher, Year of the King, 122.
7. Charles Dickens, *The Posthumous Papers of the Pickwick Club* (first published in monthly parts from April 1836 to November 1837; first published in book form November 1837. The edition quoted is from *The New Oxford Illustrated Dickens*, Oxford University Press, London, 1948), 339.
8. Hankey, *Richard III*, 61–6.
9. Sher, *Year of the King*, 168
10. Weir, *The Princes in the Tower*, 100–104.
11. Sher, *Year of the King*, 129.
12. George Gordon Byron, *The Deformed Transformed*, text quoted from *Byron, Poetical Works*, ed. Frederick Page, rev. John Jump (Oxford: Oxford University Press, 1970), 605.
13. 'Saturday, Feb. 19th', *Byron's Letters and Journals*, vol. 3, ed. Leslie Marchand (London: John Murray 1974), 244.
14. More, 21–2.
15. Sher, *Year of the King*, 26.
16. Cox, *The Lear Diaries*, 32
17. Hankey, *Richard III*, 75. Morecambe and Wise were a much loved English comic double-act, celebrated on television, especially for their 'Christmas special' shows of the 1970s.
18. More, 84. This is from the contemporary translation of More's Latin (his English version stops before this point), where the exact phrasing is 'at the draught, a convenient carpet for such a counsel'. The nature of this mockery of Richard is probably different from the expectations of modern readers; the 'groom of the chamber' – i.e., the custodian of the chamber pot – was, for obvious reasons of discretion and intimacy, the most highly placed and competitively sought after of all court positions. (For more on this, see David Starkey's *The English Court, From the Wars of the Roses to the Civil War* (London; Longman, 1987), *passim*.
19. More, 83–4.
20. Winifred H. Friedman, *Boydell's Shakespeare Gallery* (New York: Garland, 1976), 1–6.
21. Friedman, *Boydell's Shakespeare Gallery*, 61–5.

## CHAPTER 5.   MIRRORS AND SHADOWS

1. Anne Hollander, in *Seeing Through Clothes* (New York: Viking, 1978), traces the transition in Renaissance painting from small convex

hand-held mirrors – not much use to Richard here – to the large expensive wall-mirrors of Dutch interiors (pp. 392–400).

2. Cibber, *The Tragical History*, 25.

3. Peter Holland gives an account of Cibber's typical roles and stage personality in *The Ornament of Action* (Cambridge: Cambridge University Press, 1979), pointing out (pp. 90–94) that Cibber's most startling departure from playing the fop was in creating the role of the malevolent hunchback brother in Farquhar's *The Twin Rivals* (1700).

4. See Marjorie B. Garber, *Dream in Shakespeare: From Metaphor to Metamorphosis*, (New Haven: Yale University Press, 1974), 'What Freud called the "dream-work", the process by which the latent dream-thoughts are transformed into the manifest dream content, has rendered Clarence's latent suspicion of Richard, a suspicion he finds emotionally unbearable, into more reassuring terms' (p. 22).

5. Stephen Greenblatt gave an eloquent lecture on this topic at the 1998 congress of the Shakespeare Association of America (in Cleveland, Ohio), focusing on the recorded dreams of Jews under Nazism.

6. This point – and many more on the topic – is made elegantly by E. H. Gombrich in *Shadows: The Depiction of Cast Shadows in Western Art* (London: National Gallery Publications, 1995), 17–19.

7. See Victor I. Stoichita, *A Short History of the Shadow* (London: Reaktion Books, 1997), 149–52.

8. It's a recurrent idea in Jung's work, and obviously more complex than this reference suggests. For more, see *The Archetypes and the Collective Unconscious* and *Aion*, vol. 9, parts I and II, of *The Collected Works of C. G. Jung*, (New York; Bollingen Foundation Inc., 1959).

9. Berry, *The Shakespearean Metaphor*, 25: 'The shadows that visit him on the eve of Bosworth complete the play metaphor, for "shadow" can mean "actor" as well as "spirit". So the minor players in Richard's triumph return as audience to his fall.'

10. Hankey, *Richard III*, facing p. 122.

11. Leon Garfield, *Shakespeare, the Animated Tales; King Richard III* (London: Heinemann, 1994), 44.

12. Ibid, 48.

13. See Harry Levin's 'Two Tents on Bosworth Field', in *Reading the Renaissance: Culture, Poetics and Drama*, ed. Jonathan Hart (New York: Garland, 1996), 145–62.

14. Sher, *Year of the King*, 177.

15. See Edward Burns, *Character: Acting and Being on the Pre-modern Stage* (London: Macmillan 1990), 185–92.

16. See this volume, chapter 4, The Body.

17. Cibber, *The Tragical History*, 65 (F3r).

18. Hankey, *Richard III*.

19. The same thing occurs in *Julius Caesar*, when Caesar's ghost appears to Brutus (IV.iii.275).
20. See, for example, plate V of *A Harlot's Progress*, ('She Expires, While the Doctors Are Quarrelling').
21. Hammond's Arden edition, which I have followed elsewhere in this essay, has the first Quarto's 'I and I' at this point. He does not argue his choice; all the other Quartos and the Folio have 'I am I', the more usual reading in modern editions.
22. Cibber, *The Tragical History*, 67 (E4r).
23. Geoffrey Bullough (ed.) *Narrative and Dramatic Sources of Shakespeare* (London: Routledge, 1960): 'And so she putting in oblivion the murther of her innocent shildren, the infamy and dishonoure spoken by the kynge her husbande, the lyvynge in auoutrie leyed to her charge, the bastardyng of her daughters ... blynded by avaricious affeccion and seduced by flatterynge wordes, first delivered into kyng Richards handes her. v. daughters as Lambes once agayne committed to the custody of the ravenous wolfe', (p. 287).
24. Johnson takes the 'Elizabeth is persuaded' option, and responds to his own (mis?)reading thus: 'On this dialogue 'tis not necessary to bestow much criticism; part of it is ridiculous, and the whole improbable'. From *William Shakespeare, The Critical Heritage*, vol. 5 1765–74 (London: Routledge, 1979), 133. More recent critics who take the 'Elizabeth wins' option are Stephen L. Tanner, in 'Richard III v. Elizabeth: An Interpretation', *Shakespeare Quarterly*, 24 (1973), 39–47, and William B. Toole, in 'The Motif of Psychic Division in *Richard III*', *Shakespeare Survey*, 27 (1974) 21–32, where the emphasis is on Richard's psychological disintegration.
25. Weir, *The Princes in the Tower*, 76; Tey, *The Daughter of Time* (Harmondsworth: Penguin, 1951), 54.
26. Weir, *The Princes in the Tower*, 204.
27. Ibid., 179–84.
28. The historical Margaret seems to have worn a bracelet with a miniature barrel on it, to memorialize her father's fate. See Tudor-Craig *Richard III*, 82.
29. Quoted from a letter written by Peter Paul Rubens, after the death of his first wife. See Simon Sharma *Rembrandt's Eyes* (London: Allen Lane 1999), 145.

# Select Bibliography

## EDITIONS OF *RICHARD III*

Davison, Peter, *The First Quarto of King Richard III* (Cambridge: New Cambridge Shakespeare, 1996). The Quarto text, with a scholarly and well-argued introduction and notes.

Hammond, Antony, *King Richard III* (London: Arden Shakespeare, 1981). The edition used (with one slight adjustment) in this book. It is a conflation of Quarto and Folio, leaning more towards the latter. Not every choice of reading made between the two is equally convincing, but this is the fullest and most impressively thorough of editions, whose introduction includes an elegant and comprehensive account of the textual issues.

Honigman, Ernst, *Richard III* (Harmondsworth: Penguin Shakespeare, 1968). A clearly presented text, with a particularly interesting and accessible introduction. Uses the Folio more than the Quarto; perhaps less interventionist than Hammond.

Lull, Janis, *King Richard III* (Cambridge: The New Cambridge Shakespeare, 1999). One of two current Cambridge editions of the play(s), this one is based on the Folio. It gives a clear, comparatively lightly annotated text, with well-chosen theatre illustrations.

Smidt, Kristian, *The Tragedy of King Richard the Third; Parallel Texts of the First Quarto and the First Folio with Variants of the Early Quartos* (Oslo: Universitatsforlaget, 1968). Provides, very usefully, an old-spelling text of both the Quarto and the Folio, the first on the left side of an open spread, the second on the right, in the service of his highly plausible argument, as presented elsewhere, as to the identity of the Quarto, not as a 'memorial reconstruction' but as a performance text.

## SOURCES

Bullough, Geoffrey, *Narrative and Dramatic Sources of Shakespeare*, vol. 2 (London: Routledge, 1960). An invaluable anthology of the most clearly ascribable direct sources of the play, excluding, among others, More, but with an excellent introductory account of all the probable contenders.

Freeman, Thomas S., 'From Catiline to *Richard III*: The Influence of Classical Historians on Polydore Vergil's *Anglica Historia*', in *Reconsidering the Renaissance*, ed. Mario A. Di Cesare (New York: Mediaeval and Renaissance Texts and Studies, vol. 93, 1992). Traces the influence of classical historiography through Shakespeare's sources into the play.

Sylvester, Richard S., *The Complete Works of St Thomas More*, vol. 2 (New Haven: Yale University Press 1963) A notoriously biased, but rhetorically complex and extremely influential account of Richard's life and crimes.

## CRITICAL READING

The following list focuses on writing that has fed into and extends the arguments of this study.

A complete and sympathetically descriptive bibliography of all the writing on the play, up to 1986, is provided by James A. Moore in *Richard III: An Annotated Bibliography* (London and New York: Garland, 1986).

Berry, Ralph, *The Shakespearean Metaphor: Studies in Language and Form* (London: Macmillan, 1978). He points out that 'a major organising metaphor for *Richard III* is the actor, together with play/audience'.

——, *Richard III*: Bonding the Audience', in *Mirror up to Shakespeare: Essays in Honour of G. R. Hibbardd*, ed. J. C. Gray (Toronto: University of Toronto Press, 1984). Deals with the dramatist's and the audience's shared sense of space and history.

Birney, Alice Lotvin, in *Satiric Catharsis in Shakespeare: A Theory of Dramatic Structure* (Berkeley: University of California Press, 1973). Particularly good on Margaret, and on the complications of her rhetorical role.

Bloom, Harold (ed. with an introduction), *Modern Critical Interpretations: William Shakespeare's Richard III* (New York: Chelsea House Publishers, 1988). This is by far the best collection of late twentieth-century commentary on the play, with especially illuminating essays by Marjorie Garber on the relation of dreaming and the unconscious to plot and plotting (pp. 5–15), Michael Neill on mirroring and the self (pp. 15–45), and Madonne M. Miner and Marguerite Waller in feminist readings, the first focusing on the uneasy relation of the women to 'traditional' roles of wife and mother (pp. 45–60), the second a complex deconstruction of the wooing scene between

114

Richard and Lady Anne (pp. 85–100).

Campbell, Lily B., *Shakespeare's Histories: Mirrors of Elizabethan Policy* (San Marino, CA: The Huntingdon Library, 1947). A classic account of the history plays as representing a careful and conscious statement of the Elizabethan state's promotion of an idea of 'order'.

Faber, M. D, *The Design Within* (New York: Science House, 1970), 34–5. Reprints Freud's essay on the play, with other psychoanalytic accounts.

French, Marylin, *Shakespeare's Division of Experience* (New York: Summit Books, 1981), 43–75. Working from an 'essentialist' feminist perspective, reads the play in terms of Richard's violent exclusion of the feminine.

Garber, Marjorie B., *Dream in Shakespeare: From Metaphor to Metamorphosis* (New Haven: Yale University Press, 1974). A subtle, basically Freudian, account of dream in Shakespeare, focusing in the case of this play on Clarence's dream, and the role of guilt and anxiety in shaping it.

Jones, Emrys, *The Origins of Shakespeare* (Oxford: Oxford University Press, 1977). Provides a subtle and challenging reading of the history plays in relation to both humanist rhetorical traditions and the Catholic tradition of biblical drama. The chapter on *Richard III* is subtitled 'A Tudor Climax', and presents the end of the play as a kind of providential *telos*, impacting on itself Elizabeth's victory over Mary Queen of Scots, the instigation of the Tudor dynasty, and the triumph under the Roman emperor Constantine of Christianity over paganism.

Kahn, Coppelia, *Man's Estate: Masculine Identity in Shakespeare* (Berkeley: University of California Press, 1981). Focuses on the role of the family, and of 'alienation from the mother', in the formation of Richard's character, as part of a ground-breaking and still valuable study of masculinity as Shakespeare figures it within family relationship.

Kott, Jan, *Shakespeare Our Contemporary*, trans. Boleslaw Taborski (London: Methuen, 1964). A highly influential (in theatrical terms especially) and still stimulating response to the content of Shakespeare's plays from a communist bloc perspective.

Levin, Harry, 'Two Tents on Bosworth Field: *Richard III* V.iii.v', in *Reading the Renaissance: Culture, Poetics and Drama*, ed. Jonathan Hart (New York: Garland 1996). Identifies the soliloquies of *The Third Part of Henry the Sixth* as 'distinctly Marlovian', where '*Richard III* [is] more typically Shakespearean in its succinct formulation, its structural equilibrium and its psychological modality'.

Mallett, Philip, 'Shakespeare's Trickster-Kings: Richard III and Henry V', in *The Fool and the Trickster: Studies in Honour of Enid Welsford*, ed. Paul V. A. Williams (Cambridge: Cambridge University Press, 1979), 64–82. Makes a provocative link between the two kings in terms of their machiavellian tricksiness.

Muir, Kenneth, 'Shakespeare and the Tragic Pattern', *Proceedings of the British Academy*, 44 (1958), 145–62. Makes the link to 'the vice' in terms of Richard's individualism.

Righter, Anne, *Shakespeare and the Idea of the Play* (London: Chatto and Windus, 1962), 96–100. Makes the comparison to the 'vice' in connection with the theme of the 'player-king'.

Rossiter, A. P., *Angel with Horns, and other Shakespeare Lectures*, ed. Graham Storey (London: Longmans, 1961). A subtle exploration of moral ambiguity as a component of Shakespearean character.

Tillyard, E. M. W., *Shakespeare's History Plays* (London: Chatto and Windus, 1944). The classic 'conservative' account of the plays as components of an Elizabethan celebration of order.

Wilders, John, *The Lost Garden: A View of Shakespeare's English and Roman History Plays* (London: Macmillan, 1978). Largely a reaction to accounts like Tillyard's; a presentation of the darker irresolvable aspects of Shakespeare's dramatizations of history.

## THEATRICAL HISTORY

Cibber, Colley, *The Tragical History of King Richard the Third* (London, 1718; London: Cornmarket Press facsimile, 1969). A famously influential adaptation.

Colley, Scott, *Richard's Himself Again: A Stage History of Richard III* (New York: Greenwood Press, 1992) A full account of the stage history, with much American material, and the extra advantage of taking the story nearer to the present.

Cox, Brian, *The Lear Diaries: The Story of the Royal National Theatre Productions of Shakespeare's 'Richard III' and 'King Lear'* (London: Methuen, 1992). A wry, rather sceptical account of working on and touring the McKellen/Eyre production.

Garfield, Leon, *Shakespeare, the Animated Tales: King Richard III* (London: Heinemann, 1994). An elegantly expressionist 'picture book' version of the play, aimed at older children.

Hankey, Julie, *Richard III, William Shakespeare*, in the Plays and Performance series (London: Junction Books, 1981). Gives a detailed account of major performances of the play in a lively and well-sourced introduction, and in notes describing the actions of notable performers, attached to a text which conflates Folio and Quarto, but whose starting point is the Quarto-favouring 'old' Cambridge edition.

Pearson, Richard, *'A Band of Arrogant and United Heroes': The Story of the Royal Shakespeare Company Production of 'The Wars of the Roses'* (London: Adelphi Press, 1990). A short and anecdotal, but often illuminating account from an actor's point of view, of a seminal production of 'the cycle'.

Richmond, Hugh, *Shakespeare in Performance: King Richard III* (Manchester: Manchester University Press, 1989). A short comparative account of productions, predicated on an enthusiasm for the play as the climax of a 'cycle'.

Sher, Antony, *Year of the King* (London: Chatto and Windus, 1985). A highly intelligent and engagingly frank account of preparing for and performing the role by one of its most successful twentieth-century performers.

## THE HISTORICAL CONTROVERSY

Buck, George, *The History of King Richard the Third*, 1619, ed. Arthur Noel Kincaid (Gloucester: Alan Sutton 1982). One of the earliest revisionist, pro-Richard versions of the history.

Drewett, Richard, and Mark Redhead, *The Trial of Richard III* (Gloucester: Alan Sutton, 1984). The British television Channel 4 ran *The Trial of Richard III*, a court case following current British law and using all the available evidence for the historical Richard's guilt. He was found not guilty by a jury. This is a summary presentation of the proceedings.

Tey, Josephine, *The Daughter of Time* (London: Peter Davies, 1951). A witty and well-researched detective story, in which a hospitalized twentieth-century detective tries to solve the 'mystery' of the princes' murder. He finds in Richard's favour, and against Richmond/Henry VII.

Tudor-Craig, Pamela, *Richard III* (London: National Portrait Gallery, 1973). A scholarly catalogue of an exhibition of portraits of Richard and of his family.

Walpole, Horace, *Historic Doubts on the Life and Reign of King Richard the Third*, 1768, ed. P. W. Hammond (Gloucester: Alan Sutton, 1987). An elegant problematization of the 'evidence' against Richard.

Weir, Alison, *The Princes in the Tower* (London: Pimlico, 1992). A readable, full and open-minded account of the history, which nonetheless finds 'against' Richard,

## THE PLAY ON VIDEO

Not all of the following may be commercially available at any particular time, but they have all been released on video. Two of the most interesting television versions *The Age of Kings* (BBC, 1960) and *The Wars of the Roses* (Hall/Barton, RSC/BBC, 1964) have not been issued, but can be viewed by appointment at the British Film Institute and at the Shakespeare Institute, Stratford-on-Avon.

1911 *Silent Shakespeare* (BFI) includes in its compilation of early films of Shakespeare a compressed version of the play (in a version that includes the murder of Henry), acted by Frank Benson and his company, then performing both at Stratford and on tour. Not all the company have grasped the convention of silent film, but Benson himself gives a virtuoso performance of physically graphic comic villainy.

1955 Olivier's version is vividly staged in garish colour and hyperactive camera work, in a nightmare version of the middle ages influenced both by Disney and by German Expressionist film.

1982 Jane Howell's version for the BBC was the climax of a cycle of the *Henry VI* plays, using the same cast and a large stylized non-specific set throughout. It stars Ron Cook.

1990 Michael Bogdanov's English Shakespeare Company staging, with Andrew Jarvis as Richard, was filmed live at the Grand Theatre, Swansea, and issued as part of the company's complete history-cycle. It is a modern-dress version, with a sharp political, even satirical, edge.

1997 Richard Loncraine directed Ian McKellen in a reprise of his National Theatre performance, using the same idea of English fascism, and the idea of an alternative 'what if' post-war history. An insistently clever film, which could be variously claimed as either incoherent or postmodern.

## WEBSITES

This is just a selection of websites; there are currently at least twenty, a good indication of the kind of enthusiasm the subject generates.

*The Richard III Foundation* hyperlink http://www.richard111.com

*Richard III Society* – hyperlink http://home.vicnet.net.au/~richard3/welcome.htm

*Richard III Society* – hyperlink http://www.richardiii.net

*Wars of the Roses (with Richard III enthusiast page)* – www.northcoast.com/~ming/roses/roses.html

*The Richard III Online library* – hyperlink http://www.webcom.com/r3/bookcase/index.html

*The Richard III Society Online Library of Primary Texts and Secondary Sources* hyperlink – http://www.r3.org/bookcase/index.html

*The Trial of Richard III* – www.law.indiana.edu/law/realaudio/richard3.html

# Index

Note: this index does not list events or characters in the play, only the history they represent. Productions of the play discussed are indexed separately.

Stage performances of the play discussed in the text, in chronological order. The name of the actor playing Richard is given first, that of the director second.